Free in Christ

GRACE TO YOU
AND PEACE
Colossians 1: 2

By the same author:

Christmas and Epiphany
The Feast of Pentecost
Greater Things than These
Commentary on the New Lectionary (2 volumes)
The Charismatic Prayer Group
The Beginnings at Whatcombe
A People for His Praise
Pentecostal Anglicans
Live by the Spirit
The Lord is Our Healer
Prayers for Healing
Lord, Heal Me
Baptised in the Spirit?

Free in Christ

The Experience of Forgiveness

JOHN GUNSTONE

daybreak
London

First published in 1989 by
Daybreak
Darton, Longman and Todd Ltd
89 Lillie Road, London SW6 1UD

British Library Cataloguing in Publication Data

Gunstone, John, *1927–*
    Free in Christ
    1. Christian life. Forgiveness
    I. Title   II. Series
    248.4

ISBN 0–232–51803–3

Phototypeset by Input Typesetting Ltd,
London SW19 8DR
Printed and bound in Great Britain by
Anchor Press Ltd, Tiptree, Essex

Contents

Notes for discussion and a short Bible reading are
provided at the end of each chapter

Acknowledgements

I am grateful to the following for allowing me to quote from publications for which they hold the copyright: Hodder & Stoughton for the scripture quotations from the Holy Bible, New International Version (copyright © 1973, 1978, 1984 International Bible Society); Mr Edward England for the quotation from *Renewal Magazine* on pp. 41–2; J. E. Church for the quotations from his book, *Quest for the Highest* on pp. 84–5; and the General Synod of the Anglican Church in Canada for the quotation from the Book of Alternative Services 1985 on pp. 101–2.

1

The Search for Pardon

One of the first things I remember about my early school days is a lie I told to my teacher. The details of the incident have remained imprinted in my memory, even though much else about those days has been forgotten. The experience must have made a deep impression on me.

I was about seven years old. Each day in term-time I travelled on a bus from Long Eaton in Derbyshire, where my parents lived, to Breaston, a village two or three miles away, where a schoolteacher ran a small private school in a church hall. On the bus I used to sit with my friend, Tony, who got on a few stops before mine. We usually scrambled for seats on the top deck.

One day, on the journey home after school, I discovered the thrill of flipping hawthorne berries out of the bus window on to the heads of people walking on the pavement below. I urged Tony to do the same out of the next window. He looked interested for a moment, but then he shook his head.

'You shouldn't do it,' he said.

I felt piqued.

'If you don't, I won't be your friend!' I threatened.

Tony cautiously took a berry from me and threw it out of the window. At that moment the conductor came up the stairs and saw what we were doing.

'You come from Mrs Heley's school, don't you?' he said sternly.

Tony and I looked at each other guiltily.

'Well,' he went on, 'I live next door to her, and I'm going to tell her about you both when I get home tonight.'

It was bad luck we'd been caught; it was double bad luck that the conductor knew our teacher.

Next morning Mrs Heley made us both stand before her, as she demanded to know what we'd been doing.

'John started it!' blurted out Tony. 'He said if I didn't throw the berries, he wouldn't be my friend!'

I bristled with indignation.

'I didn't!' I protested.

'You did!' said Tony tearfully.

Mrs Heley looked at us reproachfully. 'One of you is lying,' she said quietly. 'Whoever it is must own up.'

Neither of us spoke. Without saying any more, she sent us back to our places. Within me was a turmoil. To begin with, I was angry with Tony for telling tales. But then remorse and shame took over. I knew I'd deliberately done something wrong. I felt wretched.

Eventually, I went to Mrs Heley and told her the truth. I remember the profound sense of relief I experienced once the confession had been made. The teacher made me apologise to Tony for implying he had lied. I don't think there were any painful consequences. Tony and I remained friends until my parents left Long Eaton a year later.

Looking back on that incident, I realise now that it signalled for me the awakening of my conscience.

Conscience is not an easy faculty to analyse. In traditional Christian teaching it has been defined as 'the mind of man making moral judgements'. Our conscience decides what is to be done or what is to be avoided in particular cases.

But our conscience is not entirely rational. Although we exercise our reason in making such judgements, our emotions are involved, too. We may feel ourselves drawn to what is good – or repelled from it, if doing what is good requires effort or courage on our part. And, of course, guilt itself is an emotion.

In the modern world the working of our conscience is generally explained by what psychologists call 'the guilt complex'. When there arises from deep within a sense of unworthiness and of separation from others, we are suffering from one of the oldest complexes known to human beings.

The guilt complex, the psychologists explain, is the action of our superego. What happens is that society, as represented by parental authority, teachers, and companions generally, imposes norms on our conduct from an early age. As children we are made to feel – since we are incapable of understanding – that certain impulses within us are forbidden. Threats are added to enforce these taboos ('Don't you dare do that again, or else. . .').

But still the impulses remain. And since young children have no idea why these particular impulses are wrong, they experience no permanent resolution of the conflict between their desire to do something and their awareness that, if they do it, they may be punished or rejected. Humanity's natural reluctance to face unpleasant truths about itself then forces down into the unconscious the memory of the forbidden desire or act. There, together with related feelings of insecurity and irrational emotions of guilt, the memory remains hidden until something causes it to well up from that pit to produce neurosis in later life.

Sociologists fill out the background picture. In different societies and at different evolutionary stages, they tell us, different norms of acceptability apply. That is why ideas about right and wrong vary between one culture and another. Hence they conclude that all norms, whatever their nature, are merely relative to the society in question.

For an example they cite the ten commandments. These primitive regulations and prohibitions, they say, are nothing more than the basic law of Israel at a certain stage of its people's historical development. The sayings were cloaked with the authority of God to make their power binding on the individual Hebrew more effective.

These explanations can be illuminating. They help us to understand the psychological mechanisms that go on inside us as we experience the pricking of our conscience. They can be valuable in assisting individuals who are crushed by an excessive sense of personal unworthiness to come to terms with themselves.

But they don't answer completely why we think and feel as we do when we know we've done something wrong. Deep within us we sense that our conscience is not just the combined influence of upbringing, environment and psychological make-up. At moments when we are able to reflect quietly on these reactions of guilt, we become aware that we are being responsive to something – or Someone – else.

To put it another way, there is a God-like quality about human beings which lifts us above the theories about who we are and why we act in the way we do. We have an instinct within us which tells us we are called to be much, much better than we are. In the classic phrase, we are 'made in the image of God'.

Sense of Sin

The scriptures tell us that, when we feel guilty, it can be because our conscience is registering the reality of sin in our lives and in the world. Through our conscience we are experiencing the truth that we belong to a human race which rejects God's will and which, as a consequence, is in a permanent and universal state of rebellion against him.

The revelation of God in the Bible's narratives of the creation and fall of man in Genesis 1–11 enables us to understand the origin of this sense of sin. Here are tales from antiquity which have become the sacred literature of Israel and through which the Holy Spirit enlightens us as to who we are and why we are alive on this planet.

When we read the stories of Adam, Cain, Noah and Babel, then, we are not just looking at a series of disconnected narratives which have evolved round figures in the past. They go much deeper than that. They describe the truth of mankind's past and present predicament, and the hope which is to come. Adam and Eve are every man and woman. We hear about Cain on most TV news programmes. Noah and the builders of the tower of Babel are ourselves in our different moods.

The stories reveal that:

(1) God created, and still sustains, the universe and gives it growth.

(2) Men and women are meant for friendship with God.

(3) Human sin (the eating of the forbidden fruit, the murder of the brother, the corruption of Noah's contemporaries, and the building of the tower) spoils both the creation God has made and the friendship men and women are meant to have with God.

(4) God does not leave men and women to their fate. He shows himself as a God of undreamed-of mercy. Every fall is succeeded by a gesture of grace.

This last point is vital. It is the prophetic insight of the book of Genesis which shows that, in each narrative, God does not allow sin to remain unchallenged in the world he has created.

When Adam and Eve were banished from the garden, they were given clothing by God, and Adam was promised that the offspring of the woman would crush the head of the serpent. Cain was given a sign that would prevent his being killed. In the story of Noah, the process of deliverance takes up most of the narrative. After Babel comes the story of Abraham, which is the beginning of the great restoration which God was to effect through his Son. Genesis not only reveals the origin of sin; it also reveals God's word that there is hope in the midst of downfall.

Later parts of the Old Testament stress the responsibility of individuals for their sins; but overall disobedience to God is presented as a collective responsibility. Sin has a power over humanity that seems to stem from humanity's very beginnings. It contaminates everything concerned with men and women, from their origins to their deaths.

Take any aspect of human creation, endeavour or relationship – the wonderful advances of science and technology; the outstanding achievements in art, sport or exploration; the dearest relationships among families and friends. Always somewhere, somehow, evil creeps in to rob them of perfection.

The psalmist expressed it:

Surely I was sinful at birth,
   sinful from the time my mother conceived me.
                                              (Psalm 51.5)

This tendency to sin came to be known in Christian theology, about the time of Augustine, Bishop of Hippo (d. AD 430), as 'original sin'. The phrase is not found in the scriptures, although the state of being in rebellion against God from the beginning – from our 'origins' (which is what 'original' sin means) – is implied in passages such as Romans 5.12, where Paul links the fact of sin with death: 'Sin entered the world through one man, and death through sin, and in this way death came to all men, because all sinned.'

Strictly speaking, original sin is not a sin at all: it is an inherent weakness in each man and woman born into this world which causes him or her, when free to choose, to choose evil. We are all in it – we are all 'in Adam' (1 Corinthians 15.22). Most of us probably know ourselves well enough to acknowledge the truth of that. We deceive ourselves if we imagine otherwise. G. K. Chesterton said that the doctrine of original sin is the only directly ascertainable doctrine of Christianity. Our condition is summed up in the general confession before morning and evening prayer in the Prayer Book when we admit 'there is no health in us'.

There is something Satanic about this tendency to sin – the cruellest of twists in the human character which tragically mars what could be so good. We are not attentive to what God wants but to what man desires. Although the possibilities of true freedom are impaired, a certain freedom still remains ours. We use it to set ourselves against God. But in so doing we lose that freedom. What we have becomes a sham. We think we're free, but we're not. We're the prisoners of sin.

In Benjamin Britten's opera, *Billy Budd*, the press-ganged young seaman is likeable and conscientious, popular with everyone from the captain down to the cabin boys. The only one on board who dislikes him is Claggart, the master-at-arms. The tragedy comes when Billy, falsely accused by Claggart of disloyalty, is unable to defend himself because of a stammer which inflicts him when he is under stress. In desperation and anger he strikes the master-at-arms with his fists, and Claggart falls down dead.

With great reluctance Captain Vere court-martials Billy and condemns him to death by hanging from the yardarm. Later, after the execution, Vere muses sadly, 'There's always a flaw in the divine image'. The opera is a moving reflection on the battle between good and evil in the world, and the truth that a seed of evil lies in the heart of what is good.

This state of being caught in the deadly infection of original sin is known as 'total depravity'. The phrase is a piece of theological jargon which is much misunderstood. Total depravity is not, and never has been, a doctrine declaring humanity to be as bad as it can be. What it does maintain is that there is an element of fallenness in all that human beings think, speak and do, and that therefore they are incapable of perfection in their own strength. This, then, is how the scriptures answer the question, 'Why do I feel so guilty when I think, say or do certain things?' It is because we are mourning for something better for ourselves, an inner awareness that we are intended to be free of the influence of those impulses and forces which drive us to wickedness. 'I have a desire to do what is good,' wrote Paul, 'but I cannot carry it out. For what I do is not the good I want to do; no, the evil I do not want to do – this I keep doing' (Romans 7.18–19).

However, a guilt complex is not another name for a sense of sin. Indeed, a guilt complex can sometimes obscure the reality of our sinfulness. It causes us to look within ourselves or at those around us, and it tempts us to seek excuses for our sinful behaviour ('I can't help it: I'm made that way'). A sense of sin, on the other hand, points us to God and leaves us with nothing to say about ourselves except that we are sinners.

Return, O Israel!

In the early centuries, sin for Israel seems to have been very close to ritual impurity, resulting in the inscrutable punishments of a 'jealous' God. But as Israel's moral consciousness advanced, the notion grew that God's law is the wise ordering of things for his people's good. By the time the books of the Law were taking their final shape, the God of the ten commandments was recognised as the God who, even before the Exodus, promised the fulfilment of his will to Abraham. Hence the law of God never becomes in the Old Testament just an impersonal word uttered from on high. It remains God's personal word addressed to his people whom he loves: 'I have called you by name.'

The relationship between God and his people was sealed in the covenant. A covenant is a bond between two parties who commit themselves to one another on a basis of personal trust. The most common use of the word today is when we agree to make a fixed donation over a number of years to a charitable cause so that the charity can recover the income tax we have paid on that sum from the inland revenue office. For this purpose we have to sign a covenant.

In making his covenant with Israel, God committed himself to the people on condition they in return committed themselves in obedience to him.

'If you obey me fully and keep my covenant, then out of all nations you will be my treasured possession' (Exodus 19.5). Israel's sin, then, was not just a matter of breaking divine laws; it was the rebellion of children against their father, or the unfaithfulness of the bride to her spouse. God's 'jealousy' is the other face of his inexplicable love for this people – all the more inexplicable because God had no need either to create men and women or to choose one nation from among them.

So Israel sought to approach God for the forgiveness of her sins. She did this particularly when illnesses and plagues, natural disasters, and attacks by enemies convinced her that she had sinned and that God in his wrath was punishing his people for their sinfulness.

To speak of Israel searching for pardon is to look at the Old Testament from a human angle – like the sociologists I mentioned earlier. Looked at with the eye of faith, the Old Testament tells us how God revealed his will to the people of his covenant and, in spite of their many backslidings, brought them to that moment in history when he manifested his love and mercy for sinners in Jesus Christ.

Pleas for mercy and forgiveness were heard frequently in the prayers and songs of Israel, as the psalms and other devotional literature of the Old Testament illustrate. Moses prayed for the forgiveness of the people after their rebellion during the exodus (Numbers 14.17–19). But the commonest way of making amends for sins was by offering sacrifices.

The most important of these was the sacrifice in Jerusalem on the Day of Atonement. 'The Day', as it came to be called, originated before the Babylonian exile. *Yom Kippur* (Hebrew, *yom hakkippurim* = 'Day of Expiations') was always observed on the 10th Tishri (September–October). The Hebrew word for atone (*kipper*) means 'to cover' or 'to blot out'. The contexts show that what is covered is the sin and, being covered, the effects of sin are removed. The eyes of God, we might say, cease to behold the offences of his people.

Directions for the observance of The Day are in Leviticus 16. Penitential exercises and fasting were enjoined, and everyone met at the temple for the special sacrifices to make expiation for the sanctuary, the priests and the people.

The climax came when two goats were brought forward. One was slaughtered and its blood sprinkled by the high priest in the holy of holies. The high priest laid his hands on the other, the scapegoat, and ritually transferred to it all the sins of the people, deliberate and accidental; then the goat was carried off into the desert and set free: 'The goat will carry on itself all their sins to a solitary place' (Leviticus 16.22).

The offering of sacrifices was interrupted during the Babylonian exile (587–535 BC) but restored after the rebuilding of the temple (516 BC). The rituals continued until Jerusalem was destroyed by the Roman general Titus in AD 70. But long before that – back to pre-exilic days – there was a growing awareness that ritual was not sufficient to assure the forgiveness of sins. What was needed was repentance and a change of heart in disobedient men and women.

In the Old Testament there are two words translated as repentance: 'to be sorry, to change one's mind', and 'to turn back, to return'.

The first is used most often of God himself, depicted in anthropomorphic terms as a man who is sorry for his people when he observes their plight or hears their expressions of regret for their sins; he

11

changes his mind about them. This is not because God himself changes but because the relationship between himself and his people changes when they repent.

The second is used of man in calls for him to repent, to return in obedience to God. Amos 4.6–11 says that the evil God intends as a consequence of Israel's sin is not malicious or vindictive, but rather is sent to bring Israel to repentance. One of the most eloquent pleas for repentance is in Hosea 14.1–2:

> Return, O Israel, to the Lord your God.
>> Your sins have been your downfall!
> Take words with you
>> and return to the Lord.
> Say to him:
>> 'Forgive all our sins
> and receive us graciously,
>> that we may offer the fruit of our lips.'

Along with these calls was the growing realisation that what is needed is a new beginning in a sinner's life, a radical change of mind and heart. Then the faithful Israelites would not only avoid sin by keeping God's law but be so transformed that their lives would reflect that law.

> I will sprinkle clean water on you, and you will be clean; I will cleanse you from all your impurities and from all your idols. I will give you a new heart and put a new spirit in you; I will remove from you your heart of stone and give you a heart of flesh. And I will put my Spirit in you and move you to follow my decrees and be careful to keep my laws.

> (Ezekiel 36.25–26)

One of the greatest passages of repentance in the Old Testament is Psalm 51. The psalmist appealed to the 'unfailing love' of God (the love of the God of the covenant) to 'blot out', 'wash away' and 'cleanse' all his sins. Then he made a full acknowledgement of his guilt:

> For I know my transgressions,
>   and my sin is always before me.
> Against you, you only, have I sinned
>   and done what is evil in your sight,
> so that you are proved right when you speak
>   and justified when you judge.
>
> (verses 3–4)

But the psalmist realised that God's pardon, wonderful as it is, does not provide the full answer to all his problems. Unless God works a radical change in him, his future would be no better than his past. Therefore he requested that God would transform the inner depths of his being so that all his thoughts and motives would be in accordance with the divine will:

> Create in me a pure heart, O God,
>   and renew a steadfast spirit within me. . .
> Restore to me the joy of your salvation
>   and grant me a willing spirit, to sustain me.
>
> (verses 10, 12)

The Spirit of God who had made man out of the dust in the beginning was summoned to do a renewing work in one who had repented and who was calling on the mercy of God.

Although the psalmist spoke for himself, his words were applicable collectively. It is likely this psalm passed into Israel's worship as a hymn of penitence for occasions such as the Day of Atonement. Certainly behind its words – as behind so many of the psalms which speak in the first person singular –

there is a vivid awareness of the community, and of speaking on behalf of that community.

When we put together the modern psychological approach to guilt and the Old Testament's faith in God as one who forgives, we have the situation which cries out for a saviour. By our disobedience, which is inherent in our human nature, we reject the love of God who made us; we ignore his will and follow our own. We also destroy that relation of sonship for which he created us.

Before we go on to see in the next chapter how God met that need in sending his Son Jesus Christ as our Saviour into the midst of our predicament, I want to recall the stages through which I experienced forgiveness in the story I told at the beginning of this chapter.

(1) I told the lie. In doing this, I committed a sin. I knew I had done something wrong in the sight of God (although my awareness of God was very undeveloped). A further – and more noticeable – effect of my sin was that it resulted in a breaking of the relationship between myself and my friend, and it gave me a sense of being isolated from the rest of the community – the teacher and the rest of the class. I felt like a leper.

(2) At first I clung to my lie and refused to own up. Pride was at work in me and I didn't want to be shown as a liar. But gradually I began to feel ashamed and sorry for my sin, realising what it was doing to me, to Tony, and to the rest of the class. I was experiencing what years later I learned was called contrition.

(3) I decided to own up to my fault. It was a complete turnaround in my attitude. I turned my back on my pride and determined to accept the

humility which this next step would involve. That was the beginning of my repentance.

(4) I owned up to the teacher. I did this because I had lied to her in the first place and it seemed right to own up to her as the leader of our little community. I made my confession to her, although it was another member of the community I had sinned against.

(5) When she had heard my confession, Mrs Heley indicated in some way that I was forgiven. In theological language, she gave me absolution. The sin no longer stood between me and her, Tony and the rest of the class.

(6) But that absolution was given conditionally. She told me I had to apologise to Tony for making him seem to be a liar. This is known as making reparation. The apology was the penance I accepted as a necessary condition for being reconciled to everyone concerned.

(7) The outcome was that all my relationships were reconciled. The memory of my sin remained – which is why I can recall it half a century later! – but it no longer affected those relationships. And if any good came out of it, it was because it taught me a little of what it means to be forgiven.

It is these stages in the process of receiving God's gift of forgiveness which we shall be discussing in this book.

For Discussion

(1) What have been the influences in forming ideas of right and wrong in your life?
(2) Can you remember when you first sensed a desire to be forgiven?

Bible Reading

Psalm 51, a prayer for forgiveness and spiritual renewal (among the categories of psalms this one is known as 'a lament').

verses 1–2   plea for mercy.

3–5   confession of psalmist that his human nature has been sinful from moment of conception in womb.

6–12   renewed prayer for deliverance. *Cleanse me with hyssop*: a reference to a purification ceremony (see Exodus 12.22).

13–17   vow to instruct others and to praise and serve God rather than to rely on the offering of sacrifices. *Bloodguilt* probably means impending death as a result of the psalmist's previous misdeeds.

18–19   a later addition, perhaps to modify the anti-sacrificial tone of the preceding verses and to adapt the psalm for use in the temple.

2

The Bringer of Forgiveness

It must have been an alarming experience. The corners of his flimsy mat were attached to ropes, and his four friends swung him over the gap they had made in the rushes of the flat roof and lowered him into the midst of the crowd in the room below.

When his mat bumped to the ground, he was lying in front of the rabbi, with the audience – religious leaders in Capernaum, some of them – looking down at him on all sides.

The rabbi spoke to him.

'Son, your sins are forgiven.'

The man on the couch was startled – and, to be honest, a little disappointed. It's good to know your sins were forgiven, he thought, but it would have been better to have been released from this awful paralysis. Besides, wasn't this chap supposed to be a healer?

Or was there some connection between his sins and his paralysis, as another rabbi had once told him?

The man on the couch didn't have an opportunity to follow up that line of thought, for the religious leaders in the audience were criticising the rabbi.

'Why does this fellow talk like that? He's blaspheming! Who can forgive sins but God alone?'

That's right, the paralysed man said to himself. The prophet has said so: 'Who is a God like you, who pardons sins and forgives the transgression of the remnant of his inheritance?' (Micah 7.18). What right has this new rabbi to say sins are forgiven?

But the rabbi was speaking again.

'Why are you thinking these things? Which is easier: to say to the paralytic, "Your sins are forgiven", or to say, "Get up, take up your mat and walk"? But that you may know that the Son of Man has authority on earth to forgive sins' – he looked down at the man lying on the ground in front of him – 'I tell you, get up, take your mat and go home.'

Unbelievingly the man moved his arms and legs. They worked! With a surge of hope, he sat up and raised himself to his feet. He could stand! Wonder and joy flooded his whole being. Hardly knowing what he was doing, he rolled up his mat, and walked out into the sunlight. He was healed!

Inside and outside the people were crying in amazement, 'We have never seen anything like this' (Mark 2.1–12).

The miracle demonstrated powerfully that Jesus Christ had come as the bringer of God's forgiveness to men and women. Sin need no longer paralyse God's people. His mercy was available for all.

When Christian artists in the early centuries depicted the ministries of the church in murals on walls, it was the healing of the paralysed man which they used to illustrate what it means to be forgiven by God.

How the gift of God's forgiveness comes to us through Jesus Christ is one of the mysteries of the Gospel. 'He has made known to us the mystery of his will according to his good pleasure, which he purposed in Christ' (Ephesians 1.9). Much is revealed to us in the scriptures, but still we only see through a glass darkly.

Mystery in modern usage means a secret or a riddle to which an answer has not been found. Thus a crime is a mystery so long as the author of it has not been discovered, but when he is discovered it is no longer a mystery.

In the New Testament 'mystery' signifies a secret which is being, or even has been, revealed, which is also divine in scope, and which can only be made known to men by God through his Spirit when he chooses to reveal it. The word is found principally in the Pauline letters, where it means God's plan of salvation which he disclosed through Jesus Christ and which is being revealed to men by his Spirit.

A mystery in this sense, then, is not to be thought of as utter unintelligibility, so that further reflection or discussion are useless. Rather, it is like a very deep well, whose waters are continuously springing up: the more that is drawn from it, the more remains to be drawn. We exercise our minds and imaginations on it, but what we learn is only what God chooses to reveal to us.

Here we are concerned with the mystery of the atonement, how it was that God made us at-one with him in Jesus Christ. We can never hope to understand what God has done and is doing for our salvation. But we can continually refresh ourselves in contemplating this mystery from the scriptures, from the church's response to it through the centuries down to the present, and from Christians' own experience of it now.

And we shall see that what is revealed by the Spirit prompts us to respond with the same awe and gratitude as those who met Jesus in his earthly ministry and received the healing and forgiveness of God through him.

So we begin by reflecting on what Jesus said and did during his ministry – particularly in what he did on Calvary – and what was revealed to the apostolic writers as they taught the first generation of believers in the years after Pentecost that their sins were forgiven.

Jesus' ministry is set against the Old Testament's understanding and practice of seeking God's pardon. The apostolic writers were very familiar with this background and they found in it concepts or themes which enabled them to receive what Christ revealed to them. As Paul wrote, 'Everything that was written in the past was written to teach us, so that through endurance and the encouragement of the scriptures we might have hope' (Romans 15.4 – Paul's 'scriptures' were, of course, what we now call the books of the Old Testament).

Three concepts or themes are used to express the meaning of Christ's life, death and resurrection for our salvation:

(1) He gave himself in an act of vicarious suffering on behalf of the people on the analogy of the figure of the Suffering Servant in Isaiah;

(2) he made a sin-offering such as had been foreshadowed in the expiatory sacrifices offered in the temple; and

(3) he manifested the reality of God's deliverance of his people from the power of sin and death.

I should say that these themes are not always distinct and separate. The apostolic writers frequently move from one to another. But we will examine them separately to appreciate how rich and varied are the biblical images through which the gift of God's forgiveness in Jesus Christ is revealed to us and to men and women of all ages.

(1) An act of vicarious suffering on behalf of the people on the analogy of the figure of the Suffering Servant in Isaiah

On several occasions during his ministry Jesus predicted his suffering and death in Jerusalem, and after his resurrection he taught his disciples that what he had endured had been foretold in the scriptures and was the means by which sins were forgiven:

> This is what is written: The Christ will suffer and rise from the dead on the third day, and repentance and forgiveness of sins will be preached in his name to all nations, beginning at Jerusalem.
>
> (Luke 24.46)

These sayings do not obviously relate to Israel's hope of a Messiah. Nowhere in the Old Testament does it say that God's 'Anointed One' (his 'Christ') would suffer. The Jews of Jesus' day certainly expected God's Messiah to come and to deliver them from the oppression of the Roman rule; but his coming was not associated with personal suffering by him. If there was to be any suffering, it would be the suffering of God's enemies when the Messiah led Israel to victory. That is why it must have shocked them when Paul preached in the synagogue in Thessalonica: 'He reasoned with them from the scriptures, explaining and proving that the Christ had to suffer and rise from the dead' (Acts 17.2–3). The passages to which Jesus must have been referring – and this is confirmed by other references in his teachings – are the songs of the Suffering Servant in the second half of Isaiah (42.1–4, 49.1–6, 50.4–11, 52.13–53.12).

Who the Servant was is not known. Some believe he was a historical figure, whose suffering and death was interpreted by the prophet as a redemptive act for the nation. Others argue that the prophet saw him as a personification of Israel, suffering exile and persecution in the working out of God's purposes. Whoever he was, the prophet's writings foretell the passion of Christ so vividly that when we read them it is difficult to believe we are not reading about Jesus himself.

The Servant was called by God to his strange and terrible mission from birth: 'He . . . formed me in the womb to be his servant, to bring Jacob back to him and gather Israel to himself' (Isaiah 49.5). Then the Songs portray his experiences:

Surely he took up our infirmities
    and carried our sorrows,
yet we considered him stricken by God,
    smitten by him, and afflicted.
But he was pierced for our transgressions,
    he was crushed for our iniquities;
the punishment that brought us peace was upon him,
    and by his wounds we are healed.
We all, like sheep, have gone astray,
    each of us has turned to his own way;
and the Lord has laid on him
    the iniquity of us all.

(Isaiah 53.4–6)

References to the Servant as being 'led like a lamb to the slaughter' (53.7) and making his life 'a guilt-offering' (53.10) set the Servant's mission in the context of the atonement sacrifices of the Jewish cult. But his personal obedience to God is the outstanding feature of the Servant's life; and it was this willing obedience to God which was demonstrated to perfection in the suffering and death of Christ.

From the moment of his conception in the womb of the Virgin Mary to his ascension, Jesus was the obedient Servant of God as well as the Son of his heavenly Father. The deliberate intention with which he set his face towards Jerusalem manifested his total obedience like that which the prophet saw in the Suffering Servant (Luke 9.51).

The mystery of the Christ who though the Son of God was also God's Servant weaves in and out of the New Testament writings. The author of Hebrews drew the two roles together in a comparison with Moses, the great servant of God: 'Moses was faithful as a servant in God's house, testifying to what would be said in the future. But Christ is faithful as a son over God's house' (Hebrews 3.5). Paul quoted the Greek version of Isaiah 53.12 when he wrote: 'He was delivered over to death for our sins and was raised to life for our justification' (Romans 4.25), perhaps echoing an early Christian confessional formula.

And the author of the fourth gospel, to whom was revealed the truth that in Jesus the Word was made flesh and dwelt among us, saw in the sacrifice of the only Son a manifestation of God's boundless love. 'For God so loved the world that he gave his one and only Son, that whoever believes in him shall not perish but have eternal life' (John 3.16).

Through sending his Son, who became incarnate as his Servant for our salvation, God out of his love provided the one who bore on our behalf all the effects of our sins and made it possible for us, through repentance and faith, to be liberated from the effects of them.

By uniting himself to our human nature and by facing triumphantly the evil of the world to the point of death, Jesus, because he is the Son and Servant of God, recreated the relationship between God and mankind which had been ruined by sin. This was Christ's service for God on our behalf: 'The Son of

Man did not come to be served, but to serve, and to give his life as a ransom for many' (Matthew 20.27).

(2) A sin-offering such as is foreshadowed by the expiatory sacrifices offered in the temple

The author of Hebrews interpreted the cross in terms of the sacrifices of Israel's cult. For him the high priests of the temple, the sin and guilt-offerings which they made on behalf of the people, and the observance of the Day of Atonement, are Old Testament 'types' – persons and practices which help us to understand what God was about in Jesus Christ. As his epistle unfolds, Christ is revealed as both the high priest and the victim of the sacrifice which makes our forgiveness possible.

Christ is high priest because, having accomplished his work on the cross and having been vindicated by the Father in his resurrection, he entered the heavens at his ascension on our behalf. He fulfilled the role of the Jewish high priest, who entered the holy of holies on behalf of the people. Also like the high priest, Jesus is our mediator and representative through whom we have access to God – an access which would otherwise be impossible for us in our sinfulness. 'Let us then approach the throne of grace with confidence, so that we may receive mercy and find grace to help us in our time of need' (Hebrews 4.16).

But Jesus did not enter the heavens with the blood of a sacrificed animal; he came to the throne of grace as the one who had offered himself as the sacrificial victim for us. It is through his blood shed on the cross that our forgiveness is made available: 'He did not enter by means of the blood of goats and calves; but he entered the Most Holy Place once for all by his own blood, having obtained eternal redemption' (Hebrews 9.12).

In the ancient world blood was regarded as the source of life, and behind the gruesome use of the blood in the rituals of the temple, the intention was to offer the life of the victim to God. The author of Hebrews acknowledged that there had been a ritual value in what was done in the temple in Jerusalem. The ceremonies had been prescribed in the law of Moses. But he knew that such sacrifices were useless for dealing with the real problem – making atonement to God for the sins of humanity. This alone was done by Jesus once and for all on the cross: 'The blood of Christ, who through the eternal Spirit offered himself unblemished to God, [will] cleanse our conscience from acts that lead to death, so that we may serve the living God' (9.14).

The offering of sacrifices implies an anxiety to propitiate the wrath of the gods, and the idea of placating a wrathful deity was dominant in the pagan cults which surrounded Israel. The Bible has a strong doctrine of the wrath of God; but that teaching is always counterbalanced by the concept of God's covenant-mercy and his loving-kindness towards his people. Rabbinic teaching just before the New Testament era was saying that the wrath of God would be revealed against his enemies on the Day of the Lord in the coming judgement, but those among his people who repented would be saved from it.

This teaching was taken up by Jesus in his warnings about persisting in sin and unbelief, and Paul echoed it when he wrote, 'The Day of the Lord will come like a thief in the night' (1 Thessalonians 5.1). But then the apostle went on, 'God did not appoint us to suffer wrath but to receive salvation through our Lord Jesus Christ' (5.9).

The word 'propitiation' is used four times in the New Testament, e.g., 'He [Christ] is the propitiation for our sins, and not for ours only, but also for the whole world' (1 John 2.2; see also Romans 3.25; Hebrews 2.17; 1 John 4.10). But the word is not used with the idea of placating a wrathful God. The Father of Jesus Christ is a loving God, and if the sinner senses his wrath, then this is because he knows that his sinfulness will separate him from God until he repents. The wrath of God, then, is the flipside of his love.

The sacrifice of Christ restores us to a loving relationship with God, in which our sins have been blotted out and are no longer held against us. In Romans Paul expounded how God had sent Christ to be an expiatory oblation for our sins: 'God presented him as a sacrifice of atonement through faith in his blood' (3.25). Hence 'we have now been justified by his blood' (5.9). To be 'justified' is to be accounted righteous by God, so that we are no longer separated from him by our disobedience.

From the Reformation onwards theologians have debated how 'being justified' is to be understood. Are we accounted righteous before God in the sense of being acquitted, as in a court of law? Or does God make us righteous by infusing his grace into us so that we are truly righteous through and through? Recent ecumenical conversations – notably those of the Anglican Roman Catholic International Commission in their report, *Salvation and the Church* (1986) – acknowledge that there is truth on both sides of the argument. But what is unquestioned is that the initiative always lies with God. There is nothing we can do to earn or to merit our salvation. We are reconciled to God because God in his love wishes us to be.

This is the radical difference between the Old

Testament and the New Testament. In the Old Testament men are said to make atonement for sin, especially in the sacrifices they offered. But in the New Testament such an idea is unthinkable. It is God alone, God in Christ, who makes reconciliation possible. So at the heart of the Gospel is this message of reconciliation. That was what was promised when the apostles preached Jesus Christ: 'Repent and be baptised, every one of you, in the name of Jesus Christ for the forgiveness of your sins. And you will receive the gift of the Holy Spirit' (Acts 2.38). On the day of Pentecost Peter was exhorting the crowds in Jerusalem to be reconciled with God, and the church has continued to proclaim this message of reconciliation ever since. We shall see later that faith in God's reconciling power is the key to the church's understanding of her mission.

Once God has reconciled us to himself, then we experience the peace which God gives to those who are united with him. What comes into our lives is an inner sense that, provided we are always repentant for our wrongdoings and seeking to make amends, there is an inner assurance we are no longer separated from our heavenly Father – whatever happens to us. And since Christ by his death has brought to us the peace of God, we can now live at peace with all men (Romans 5.1, 12.8).

Moreover, sinners who repent need no longer fear the wrath of God's judgement on them; they are the recipients of God's love. 'In this is love, not that we loved God, but that he loved us and sent his Son to be the expiation for our sins' (1 John 4.10 RSV). The same thought is in Paul: 'Since we have now been justified by his blood, how much more shall we be saved from God's wrath through him' (Romans 5.9).

The sacrificial animal most closely linked with

Jesus was the lamb, the centre of the Passover celebrations, as we will see in a moment. Abraham, whose willingness to offer his only son, Isaac, was seen as a 'type' of Christ's sacrifice, had prophesied that God would provide a lamb for the burnt-offering (Gen 22.8).

The giving of blood in order to save life is a common practice in modern medicine. I met a friend recently whose son has been ill for many years. In spite of his disabilities, however, the boy has done well at school. The father told me that his son's kidneys had ceased to function properly just as the boy was about to enter university.

'I'm giving him one of my kidneys later this year,' my friend went on. 'I have to give him some of my blood first, and then the operation will go ahead if everything is satisfactory.'

No human achievement can ever match the mystery of God's saving act in Jesus Christ. But as I wondered at the love and self-sacrifice of that father (and of others who make donations of a similar kind), it struck me that what I was hearing was a tiny parable of our redemption through the blood of Jesus Christ.

(3) A manifestation of divine deliverance from the power of sin and death

Redemption is a strange word to us who have no experience of the slave-markets of the ancient world. But in our Lord's time everyone knew what it meant when a slave was redeemed. It happened when he was able to purchase his right to become a free man, or when a benefactor did that for him. In the latter case, the benefactor was known as the slave's redeemer.

Similar transactions sometimes took place in the

case of prisoners or hostages held by an enemy. This is closer to our experience, for the abominable practice of hostage-taking by terrorists on aircraft and elsewhere is well known. When we have watched on our television screens the long-drawn-out process of negotiations with those who have hijacked an aircraft with its helpless passengers, we have seen an act of redemption being performed.

In the Old Testament God was revealed as Israel's Redeemer. The escape from Egypt was one of his great acts of redemption, saving the whole nation from slavery. This was celebrated each year at the feast of the Passover (Exodus 12. 3f, 11, 14). The Babylonian captivity was another. The prophet pictured the people returning to Jerusalem along the Way of Holiness after they had been freed:

Only the redeemed of the Lord will walk there,
    and the ransomed of the Lord will return.
They will enter Zion with singing;
    everlasting joy will crown their heads.
                              (Isaiah 35.9–10)

By the New Testament era rabbis were teaching that God's final redemption of his people would come at the end of time. Then the Anointed One of God would arrive from heaven to vindicate his people. Devout Jews, like Simeon and Anna, prayed for that coming redemption (Luke 2.38).

Jesus' ministry, culminating in his death, resurrection and ascension, was revealed in the New Testament as the great and final Passover for the redemption, not just of Israel, but for all those who repented and believed in him.

The last supper was either a Passover meal or a meal associated with that celebration (the fourth gospel makes it the former; the synoptic gospels the latter), and Jesus sealed this connection by a command which would make the supper of the Lord a focus of the church's worship for ever afterwards.

The Lord Jesus, on the night he was betrayed, took bread, and when he had given thanks, he broke it and said, 'This is my body, which is for you; do this in remembrance of me.' In the same way, after supper he took the cup, saying, 'This cup is the new covenant in my blood; do this, whenever you drink it, in remembrance of me.'

(1 Corinthians 11.23–25)

When the Israelites celebrated the Passover round the table with the lamb, bitter herbs and cups of wine, they did it in remembrance of the redemption God had achieved for them at the time of Moses. The Passover of Christ is celebrated by Christians everywhere today in remembrance of the redemption he has won for us on the cross.

The fourth gospel underlines this connection by introducing Jesus as the Lamb of God who takes away the sins of the world (John 1.29, 36) and by setting his ministry of Jesus within a chronological framework of three successive Passover festivals (2.13; 6.4; 11.55). According to this evangelist, the crucifixion took place on the day before the Passover when the lambs were slaughtered in preparation for the feast (John 19.14), and on the cross Jesus died like a Passover lamb without a bone being broken (19.36 'not a bone broken' = Exodus 12.46 and Numbers 9.12).

The blood of the original Passover lambs had saved the people in Egypt from the angel of death and made the exodus possible for them. In the same way the blood of Christ in his great Passover made it possible for God's people to be freed from the slavery of sin and death and to enter the promised land of his kingdom.

The theme of our redemption in Christ's victory passed into the teaching of the apostolic church. It was revealed that God's people were redeemed, delivered from bondage and constituted as a people for God's own possession (Acts 20.28; Ephesians 1.14; 1 Peter 2.10; Titus 2.14).

God through Moses had established the old covenant on Sinai. Now through the death of Christ God was making a new covenant with his people, replacing the old, broken covenant. Like Moses, Christ is the mediator of that new covenant (Hebrews 8.6; 9.15; 12.24) – the 'one mediator between God and man' (1 Timothy 2.5). The prophecy of a new covenant between God and his people was foretold by Jeremiah 31.31–34. The only place in the New Testament where this passage is extensively quoted is in Hebrews 8.8–12, where the author points out that the Sinai covenant has been replaced by a 'better covenant'. Christians are the servants of the new covenant (2 Cor 3.6, see 1 Cor 11.25; Luke 22.20) and their sacred writings the books of the 'new testament'.

In the Book of Revelation Christ is the sacrificial lamb who has freed us from our sins by his blood (5.6; see 1.5 and 7.14); but through his victory on the cross he is not only a Passover lamb but also a military, conquering lamb, who goes forth to fight the enemies of the flock at the head of fighting rams (a picture from Jewish apocalyptic literature).

They [the kings and the beast to whom they give authority] will make war against the lamb, but the lamb will overcome them because he is Lord of lords and King of kings – and with him will be his called, chosen and faithful followers.

(Revelation 17.14)

These, then, are the three main themes through which the mystery of God's saving work in Jesus Christ was revealed to the apostolic church. By reflecting on them in the infinite variety of ways in which they are presented to us in the scriptures and in Christian tradition – and particularly in the church's liturgy – the light beyond the glass through which we see darkly is brightened. The wonder of what God has achieved for us grows.

It is through faith in this doctrine of the atonement that the church has preached the Gospel of forgiveness ever since. And it is the practical outworking of that faith which we must now examine.

For Discussion

(1) What do the titles of Jesus as 'Lord' and 'Saviour' mean to you in the practical business of everyday living?
(2) Which of the three themes of Christ's saving work outlined in this chapter do you find most helpful?

Bible Reading

Romans 6.1–14

verses 1–4 *Shall we go on sinning. . . ?* Apparently some had objected to Paul's teaching of justification by faith because they thought it would lead to moral irresponsibility. *Buried with him through baptism*: baptism of believers normal in NT church. *Through the glory of the Father*: glory is a divine attribute which also manifests the power of God.

5–10 *Our old self*: what we once were, unregenerate. *Body of sin*: pre-Christian state. *Has died*: with Christ to power of sin.

11–14 *Count yourselves*: believe this about yourselves. *Parts of your body*: all the various capacities you have as a human being.

3

The Forgiven Community

So far we have been discussing sin:

(1) as an act of disobedience to God, our Father, whose love we reject when we ignore his will and follow our own; and

(2) as a destruction of our sonship, since when we sin we are refusing the condition on which our sonship is based – a loving and obedient response to that love.

There is, however, a third dimension of sin which we need to recognise:

(3) as an offence against all the members of God's family – those who are in Jesus Christ through repentance, faith, baptism and the gift of the Holy Spirit.

We can understand the first two dimensions. Disobedience is something we are all familiar with! So, too, is the destruction of a relationship. We know what it's like to have offended someone and to sense that separation from them which exists until we have apologised.

But we question the third dimension. How can my sin, personal and sometimes secret as it is, offend every other church member? How can I be separated from them if they don't know anything about it?

It's a puzzle for us because we fail to appreciate

what the church really is and why our salvation is so intricately involved with membership of it.

We live in a very individualistic age. 'What I do is my affair and nobody else's' is a common assumption. We've so stressed the freedom of the individual that we've lost much of the sense of community which has been – and still is – a characteristic of most other cultures.

Our Western Christianity – and especially those spiritualities which stem from the Reformed tradition, including Anglicanism – has taught us a very individualistic concept of salvation. Repentance and faith are my business and no one else can repent or believe for me. Full stop!

The combined effect of this religious and cultural environment causes us to miss the fundamental truth that what our Lord has done and continues to do for us, he does because we are one in him together. Therefore what affects my relationship with God also affects my relationship with the rest of his family.

The message of the Gospel is that we don't have access to God apart from the community of his people. Once we have made our decision for Jesus Christ, we are intimately involved with those other people who have repented and believe as well.

The New Testament reveals that those who are in union with Jesus Christ are also in union with those who are his disciples. In the Acts of the Apostles, the phrase 'one another' occurs over and over again. The earliest picture we have of the church is that of a company of people whose unity was outstanding: 'All the believers were one in heart and mind' (Acts 4.32).

The truth of this impressed itself on me when in the early 1970s I spent four years with a small Christian community, the Barnabas Fellowship at Whatcombe House in Dorset. There about a dozen of us lived together as an extended family, sharing our lives and ministering to those who came and stayed with us as guests.

Those four years provided me with a completely new experience of what it means to be the church. There the great biblical metaphors of the people of God – the bride of Christ, the vine, the family of God, the flock of the good shepherd, the body of Christ – came alive for me more than they had ever done while I was a member of an ordinary congregation. It was among my friends in the Fellowship that I learned what it means to be a community with the diversities of spiritual gifts (Romans 12.4–8; 1 Corinthians 12.12ff). It was also there that I came to see, as I'd never done before, that to describe the church as the body of Christ is another way of affirming Jesus' charge to his disciples, 'A new command I give you: Love one another. As I have loved you, so you must love one another. By this all men will know that you are my disciples, if you love one another' (John 13.34–35).

Because it was such a loving community, it was soon evident to me that my faults had knock-on effects among the others. I could not be bad tempered, or slack, or critical – indeed, anything sinful – without my attitudes, words and actions having their effect on the rest of the Fellowship. In a congregation my failings were not always so obvious (or so it seemed!). But at Whatcombe it was quite different.

The experience made sense of the way in which Paul employed the metaphor of the body of Christ to teach the disastrous effects of disobedience to God among the members of the church. Unrepented sin is like an infection in a part of the human body: 'If one part suffers, every part suffers with it'

(1 Corinthians 12.26). We cannot rid ourselves of this mutual responsibility and interdependence: 'For none of us lives to himself alone and none of us dies to himself alone. If we live, we live to the Lord; and if we die, we die to the Lord. So, whether we live or die, we belong to the Lord' (Romans 14.7–8).

A simple contemporary analogy would be a team of players in a football match. The success of the team depends on every member playing to the best of his ability until the final whistle is blown. If one player is not giving his best to the game, then his neglect affects the whole team. This is true whether or not the rest of the team realise what is happening. Similarly, my sins, whether they are public or secret, affect the other members of the church.

To be disobedient to God, then, is to sin against our sisters and brothers in Christ as well.

This truth is dramatically demonstrated in the story of Ananias and Sapphira in the book of Acts. This episode is so important in what it reveals on the relationship between personal sin and church membership that we must look at it in some detail.

Separation and Death

To appreciate its implications we have to look back to the tale of Israel's entry into the promised land. The invasion by the tribes over the river Jordan was regarded as a holy war (similar to the attitude of present-day militant Islamic states in combating their enemies). In this war the real commander of the army was the Lord himself – Joshua, Moses' successor, was simply the Lord's earthly lieutenant – and the campaign had to be conducted exactly as the Lord prescribed. To ignore the divine commander's instructions was sacrilegious and therefore a grave sin.

One of those instructions was that the cities taken by the Israelites were to be 'devoted to the Lord' with their inhabitants and their goods (Joshua 6.17). This meant that they had to be totally destroyed and burned or buried. Appalling as this is to us today, for the Old Testament chroniclers it was a sign that the enemy, his households and his possessions were being handed over to God in the way all sacrifices were handed over – by destruction. None of the Israelites was to profit personally from the holy war by capturing slaves or taking booty.

Jericho was 'devoted to the Lord' by destruction after it had fallen, except for Rahab and her household, who had served the Lord by sheltering the Israelite spies. But when the assault on the next city, Ai, failed, it was revealed to Joshua that the defeat had been brought about because Achan had sinned by keeping some of the plunder from Jericho hidden in his tent. The divine commander's instructions had been ignored, and Achan's disobedience had weakened the fighting power of the Israelites. The people were only cleansed when Achan, his household and his possessions had been destroyed and buried. Once that was done, Ai fell.

The parallel was probably in Luke's mind as he wrote the book of Acts. He described how after Pentecost the new Israel was launched into a holy campaign for the Gospel of the kingdom. In spite of the growing opposition of the enemies of that Gospel, the Jewish authorities, the young church was astonishingly successful. It was also, as we've just noted, a very united body, sharing all things in common.

Then sin crept into the holy company. By cheating, as Achan had done, Ananias and his wife,

Sapphira, denied this unity. Their offence was hypocrisy, a sin which received from Jesus the most scathing condemnation. Ananias alleged that all the money he had obtained from selling a possession was given to the common purse, whereas in fact he had retained part of it for his own use.

The couple's sin was discerned by Peter: 'Satan has so filled your heart that you have lied to the Holy Spirit.' They had not only offended against God but also against the community, who derived its unity and strength from the Holy Spirit. And when charged by the apostle, they dropped down dead (Acts 5.1–17).

Whatever the historical facts are behind this story, it is evident that in the memory of the early church Ananias and Sapphira were a couple who sinned so grievously that they had to be separated from the community in order that its membership might be cleansed. Outside its fellowship was spiritual death.

This act of separation is known as 'excommunication'. To our ears it sounds like being barred from receiving the bread and the wine at the eucharist; but its true meaning is 'being made ex-community' – that is, excluded from the Christian fellowship. The withholding of communion is an outward manifestation of that.

Traces of this discipline are found elsewhere in the New Testament. Paul ordered the church in Corinth to excommunicate a member who was guilty of immorality: 'Hand this man over to Satan, so that the sinful nature may be destroyed and his spirit saved on the day of the Lord' (1 Corinthians 5.5).

The phrase, 'handed over to Satan', may have been a piece of ecclesiastical jargon, for it is also used in 1 Timothy 1.20. The idea behind it is that, outside the Christian fellowship, the sinner would be more exposed to attacks of Satan and therefore would, it was hoped, be brought to repentance in time for the Lord's second coming.

The church is to be a 'holy nation' (1 Peter 2.9), and her members have to be cleansed, not only in their personal lives, but also in their corporate life. The one who refuses to repent of his or her sin must be separated from the rest of the body.

The sense of the individual sinner contaminating the holy people of God is brought out in Paul's explanation to the Corinthians about why they must expel the unrepentant member of their congregation.

'Don't you know,' he asked them, 'that a little yeast works through the whole batch of dough? Get rid of the old yeast that you may be a new batch without yeast – as you really are. For Christ, our Passover lamb, has been sacrificed' (1 Corinthians 5.6–7).

The reference is to the ritual cleansing of the Israelite household before the celebration of the Passover. All remains of yeast were removed by the mother of the family because leavened bread was regarded as impure. Unleavened bread was used, as in the exodus. The unrepentant sinner, then, was like a piece of yeast or leavened bread remaining in the household of the church: he had to be got rid of to cleanse the church and prepare her for celebrating her redemption through the Passover of Christ.

The discipline of excommunication has been exercised throughout the history of the church in a variety of ways. One of the most famous occasions was the excommunication of Henry II after the murder of Thomas Becket, Archbishop of Canterbury, in his cathedral in 1170. It was only lifted after the king had made an act of penance at the archbishop's tomb four years later.

In England traces of this discipline remained right

up to the latter half of the nineteenth century. An elderly priest I know tells me that when his mother was a little girl in Colchester, Essex, in the 1870s, she was not allowed to go to church one Sunday because a woman was doing penance.

The woman had to stand in the midst of the church wearing a white sheet while the preacher expounded on the enormity of her sin (bearing an illegitimate child) and prayers were said for her. No wonder the church eventually dropped the practice!

The rules about excommunication remain in most of the denominations of the west in some form or other, but they are either dead letters or ineffective. The Roman Catholic bishops in Ireland have excommunicated all those associated in any way with the IRA, but that has not stopped some of their clergy from presiding at the funerals of terrorists.

In other parts of the world – and especially where there are movements of spiritual renewal – the discipline is still applied. Edward England has described how he and his wife had visited the Hope of Bangkok Church in Thailand. The pastor of this church is Dr Kriengsak Charoenwongsak, and the congregation, meeting in a converted cinema, consists of 1800 people, most of them young and seventy per cent of them new Christians.

> The Sunday service, for the benefit of visitors, was translated simultaneously into English and Chinese, and with a 60-minute Bible study that was appreciated. It was not, however, the sermon I recall but the expulsion that morning from church membership of seven Christians who had sinned and not repented. Their names and offences – adultery, stealing, etc. – were read out and they were publicly removed from the church register. It was a rare occurrence and a painful

one. Prolonged pastoral counselling had preceded it, with repeated opportunities for repentance, but the church's testimony could not be allowed to suffer by keeping them on the membership role. Later I questioned Dr Kriengsak about it. 'Part of the agreement,' he said, 'when one becomes a member of the Hope of Bangkok Church, is a willingness to accept the discipline. With love we remove from membership those who refuse to turn from their sin, and one day we hope to welcome them back into fellowship. We never ask anyone to leave because they have sinned but when they will not repent. There can be no respect for Christianity in Thailand unless we are serious about the standards.'
(Renewal Magazine, no. 134, July 1987, pp. 8–9).

Reunion and Life

However, the church not only separates the sinner from her membership. She proclaims the gift of God's forgiveness and declares that forgiveness in the power of the Holy Spirit for those who repent.

This does not mean that Christians, either individually or corporately, have any power to forgive sins themselves. Those who criticised Jesus' words to the paralysed man were right when they asked, 'Who can forgive sins but God alone?' But the union of Jesus Christ with his church is such that the church, when acting in accordance with his will, proclaims the absolution of sins in his name in appropriate circumstances.

The authority for this declaration of God's forgiveness is spread over a number of New Testament passages.

There are the records of the commissioning given

by Jesus to his disciples. The first occurs after the confession of Peter: 'I will give you the keys of the kingdom of heaven; whatever you bind on earth will be bound in heaven, and whatever you loose on earth will be loosed in heaven' (Matthew 16.19). The words are repeated in Matthew 18.18 in the context of dealing with a member who sins against a brother and refuses to be reconciled.

The exegesis of this passage is not easy. It has been so notoriously abused in the past to justify the exercise of almost any form of ecclesiastical power that it is difficult for us to approach it in a fresh way. Obviously it cannot mean that the ultimate decision about an individual's eternal destiny is decided only by fellow men and women.

But there is a consensus among all Christians that, when acting under the guidance of the Spirit, the church is able to determine when a unrepentant sinner should be 'bound' (put under the discipline of being excluded from the sacramental life of the fellowship) and when a penitent sinner should be 'loosed'. Reference to 'in heaven' in Matthew is a circumlocution for describing God's action.

The second record of the commissioning is in the resurrection appearance in the fourth gospel: 'Jesus said, "Peace be with you! As the Father has sent me, I am sending you." And with that he breathed on them and said, "Receive the Holy Spirit. If you forgive anyone his sins, they are forgiven; if you do not forgive them, they are not forgiven' (John 20.21–22).

God does not forgive people's sins because we do, nor does he withhold forgiveness because we withhold it. What Jesus meant was that, when the disciples embarked on their mission proclaiming the Gospel, there would be those who would repent and whose sins would be forgiven, and there would be those who would not repent and whose sins would not be forgiven. In the power of the Holy Spirit they would be able to discern this and announce the forgiveness or the retention of sins in Jesus' name.

The same charge is found in Luke 24.47: 'Repentance and forgiveness of sins will be preached in his name to all nations, beginning at Jerusalem.'

The first way the church fulfils this commission is in baptism. When we are baptised, we repent of our sins and are joined with the crucified and risen Lord who has conquered sin and death. Of course, baptism means other things as well – it incorporates us into Christ, it makes us members of the church, it offers us the gift of the Holy Spirit. But all this is based on the forgiveness of our sins through the new covenant of Jesus Christ.

But the New Testament church soon discovered that those who were baptised were not thereby shielded from further temptations or prevented from falling into further sins. Besides telling us about Ananias and Sapphira, Luke was remarkably open in revealing the failings as well as the achievements of the early church. There were squabbles between the Hebraic and Grecian Christians on the treatment of widows (6). There was Simon Magus' attempt to purchase divine power (8.18–24). There was the quarrel between Paul and Barnabas (15.36–41).

The apostolic letters reveal the same picture. We happen to know about the situation in Corinth because Paul's first letter to that church mentioned a number of its faults – jealousy, strife, division, immorality, a court case between two members, disorder at worship, pride in and misuse of spiritual gifts, and false teaching about the resurrection. Although we do not have so much information about the other churches, we get the impression they were not so very different from the warnings Paul and other apostolic writers issued. The same impression is given in the letters to the seven churches in Asia in the book of Revelation.

Although on the one hand the New Testament presents the church of Jesus Christ as one with her Lord – washed and sanctified by his Spirit – yet on the other hand it is only too obvious that her members were still liable to fall into sin under the influence of the world, the flesh and the devil.

When people say they wish that the present-day church was more like the New Testament church, I'm tempted to point out that in many ways it isn't really so different! Martin Luther summed up the situation in his well-known dictum: *simul justus et peccator* ('both righteous and sinful').

Members of the church who repented were pronounced forgiven by God and welcomed back into the fellowship. The authority to forgive sins committed before baptism was applied to sins committed after baptism as well. In fact, in the first centuries of the church this declaration of forgiveness was known as 'a second baptism'.

There is only one clear example of this in the New Testament. It appears in the second letter Paul wrote to his troublesome congregation in Corinth: 'Now . . . you ought to forgive and comfort him, so that he will not be overwhelmed by excessive sorrow. I urge you, therefore, to reaffirm your love for him' (2 Corinthians 2.6–8).

Paul was not exercising his apostolic authority in this case; he was asking the church to receive the sinner back into its fellowship once more. Who this sinner was we do not know for certain. Some think he was the immoral man who was excommunicated in 1 Corinthians 5. Nor do we know if the Corinthians did as Paul requested. But the passage reveals that besides excluding sinners from the community the New Testament church believed it was God's will that those who repented should be received back again as well.

Warnings

Not everyone who sinned was excommunicated. Some were to be patiently warned (1 Thessalonians 1.14); others to be gently restored (Galatians 6.1); the idle were to be shunned for a time (2 Thessalonians 3.14–15). It was only those who persistently refused to repent who were put out of the community. A procedure for dealing with these offenders was laid down in Matthew 18.15–18; the sinner who refused to be reconciled with another privately or after appearing before the leaders of the church was to be treated as a pagan or a tax collector (two characters who were regarded as outside the covenant of God).

Along with this discipline were lists of sins with warnings of the consequences of persisting in such wickedness: 'I warn you . . . that those who live like this will not inherit the kingdom of God' (Galatians 5.21; see also Romans 1.29; 2 Corinthians 12.20; Ephesians 5.3; Colossians 3.5; 1 Peter 4.3; Revelation 21.8). Those who do not repent of immorality, covetousness, idolatry, uncleanness, and other faults listed are not the people over whom God rules as king.

Inevitably this gave rise to the question of what kind of offence was regarded as so serious that the offender should be excommunicated. No clear answer to this appears in the New Testament, though we note that other sinners in Acts, such as Simon the Sorcerer (8.18–24), were disciplined but not excommunicated. There was no suggestion that either Paul or Barnabas should be put out of the fellowship after they had quarrelled!

The nearest we get to a division between grave sins and less grave ones comes when the question of admitting Gentiles to the church was being settled. Then the council of apostles and elders in Jerusalem laid down that certain offences could not be tolerated: 'It seemed good to the Holy Spirit and to us not to burden you with anything beyond the following requirements: You are to abstain from food sacrificed to idols, from blood, from meat of strangled animals and from sexual immorality' (Acts 15.28–29).

Although modern commentators have had difficulty in deciding what the second prohibition means (could it mean the consumption of blood in meat, forbidden in Leviticus 17.10–12, or the shedding of blood by murder?), the early church had no doubt that apostasy, murder and immorality were particularly grave sins for which a member was excommunicated until he or she had repented and been reconciled.

In later Christian moral teaching the sins listed in the New Testament came to be known as 'mortal', because it was believed their effect on the Christian was spiritual death – they cut him off from the eternal life of Christ unless he repented. The so-called seven deadly sins were a summary taken from the lists. They are remembered by the mnemonic, PLAGUES = P, pride; L, lust; A, avarice; G, gluttony; U (double U = W!), wrath or anger; E, envy; S, sloth. (Contrast these with the seven virtues, or fruit of the Spirit, of Galatians 5.22–23.) Lighter offences came to be known as 'venial'.

We also find in the New Testament traces of a conviction that certain sins could not be declared forgiven because they were so grave they had to be left to the mercy of God. This seems to be the background to 1 John 5.16, 'There is a sin that leads to death' (see Hebrews 6.4–6; 10.26). Associated with these passages is Jesus' warning, 'Whoever blasphemes against the Holy Spirit will never be forgiven; he is guilty of an eternal sin' (Mark 3.29; see Matthew 12.31–32; Luke 12.10).

In the early centuries the church thought these passages meant that apostasy was not to be absolved. But this rigorism dissolved when it was clear that many of those who had sacrificed to the Roman emperor were truly penitent and were seeking readmission to the Christian fellowship (as we shall see in the story of Serapion in Chapter 6). In any case, the church always read in the scriptures the example of Peter, who denied his Lord three times on the night of the crucifixion, but a few days later was welcomed to breakfast by the side of the lake by the risen Christ (John 21.12).

The 'sin against the Holy Spirit' is the ultimate and deliberate rejection of God's goodness; it is to ascribe to Satan what is manifestly the work of God – a state of mind which, so long as it lasts, is essentially unforgivable and might easily become permanent.

So the church has exercised the power to bind and to loose in different ways in different ages and cultures. One example can be seen in the church's attitude towards the remarriage of divorced persons during the lifetime of the previous partner.

A century or so ago, remarriage after divorce was considered such a grave sin that the couple were automatically excommunicated, at least for a time. (In the Roman Catholic Church that did not apply if the previous marriage was annulled – that is, declared not to have been a real marriage.) The ban also meant that such second marriages could not be solemnised in a church service.

In the last fifty years or so, however, with more marriages ending in divorce, the church's attitude has gradually softened. Such couples are no longer automatically excommunicated, and in many denominations their marriages take place in a church service.

Such an example reminds us that the exercise of the ministry of reconciliation by the church is always provisional. Only God knows what is in the hearts of men and women who fall into sin and then repent. The prayers which absolve the sinner can never be anything other than a hope of what we trust in the infinite mercy of God.

What matters for us is the genuineness of our repentance.

For Discussion

(1) When and where did you experience the closest Christian fellowship?
(2) What, in your opinion, distinguishes a grave sin from a lighter one?

Bible Reading

John 13.1–17

verses 1–5   *The Father had put all things under his power*: the fourth gospel emphasises that Jesus had control of every situation and that he was fulfilling God's purposes. *Began to wash his disciples' feet*: a menial duty usually performed by a slave; it was a lesson in selfless service to others, which in Jesus' case would lead to the cross (Luke 22.27).

6–11 *No, you shall never wash my feet*: was Peter's objection due to his pride or his humility? *Not just my feet but my hands and my head as well!* Peter was still dictating what Jesus should do. *Only to wash his feet*: a bath can be taken before a meal.

12–17 *Teacher* and *Lord*: both instructor and master.

4

Repentance

One of the obvious – but often overlooked – essentials about forgiveness is that it is a gift. For-*give*-ness. The same root meaning is in the alternative word, pardon. This is the English version of the Old French word, *pardoner*, itself derived from the Latin, *(per)donare*, to give. Forgiveness is the act whereby an injured party allows the party responsible for the injury to go free. What is due to the injured one for the injury is waived aside as the gift to the one responsible.

The New Testament teaches that God takes upon himself the act of reparation, so that we may be restored to a true relationship with him. The discussion in Chapter 2 sketched how the Father did this through his Son by the power of his Spirit. He thereby made it possible for us to respond to his love and live in obedience to him. On our side we have to be repentant.

You sometimes hear it said that forgiveness is conditional upon our repentance. But we need to be careful how we use the word 'conditional'. It is certainly not right to use it in relation to God's love, which is wholly unconditional. It is better to say that God's love calls forth repentance out of our hearts, rather as the light and warmth of the sun bring new life out of a plant.

God's gift of forgiveness is not dependent on our repentance. He does not, as it were, strike a bargain with us: If you repent, I will pardon you. That is not a relationship of love. What God offers us is a new kind of fellowship with him which is individual, personal and decisive, and which is completely unmerited and undeserved.

This is very different from what many people, particularly non-Christians, say today. They tell us that we must help people to forgive themselves. Usually this means that we are expected to condone a sin or a series of sinful attitudes and acts.

Now although there may be some who, as part of the process of healing, have to be released from a morbid self-hatred or sense of unworthiness, it is unloving to pretend that sins do not exist. It leaves the sinner in a worse state than before. And since only God can forgive sins, it is necessary that a sinner faces up to his or her faults and repents.

The lesson is in the parable of the two men, the Pharisee and the tax collector, who went into the temple to pray. It contains one of the starkest contrasts in all the tales Jesus told.

The Pharisee's prayer wasn't really a prayer at all: it was a self-eulogy which revealed only his pride in his own righteousness and religious achievement: 'God, I thank you that I am not like other men – robbers, evildoers, adulterers – or even like this tax collector. I fast twice a week and I give a tenth of all I get.' With those few words Jesus conveyed the impression that robbers, evildoers and adulterers would be quite nice people to meet compared with this Pharisee!

The tax collector, on the other hand, stood at a distance. 'He would not even look up to heaven, but beat his breast and said, "God, have mercy on me, a sinner".' For all his faults and follies, the tax collector thought only of God; and because his mind was on God, he knew himself to be a sinner. He did the only thing that God required of him: faced the truth about himself, confessed himself to be a sinner, and cast himself upon God's compassion.

We are not at all surprised when Christ ends his parable with the comment, 'I tell you that this man, rather than the other, went home justified before God. For everyone who exalts himself will be humbled, and he who humbles himself will be exalted' (Luke 18.11–15).

We need to remember that repentance is not a degrading business, like rubbing our noses in the mud. Repentance is the key which enables us to enter into the freedom and joy which Jesus longs to give us as the bringer of forgiveness.

Faith and repentance go together, because it is as we become aware of who Jesus Christ is that we also become aware of what we need through him. The Holy Spirit both enlightens our minds and hearts with the truth of the Son of God, and convicts us of our sinfulness. While we tell ourselves that we are good people and have no need of repentance, the gift of forgiveness cannot be received by us from God.

We see this response of faith and repentance in some of those individuals who came in contact with Jesus Christ during his earthly ministry.

One outstanding example was that of Peter. After seeing the miracle of the draught of fishes, he suddenly became conscious that the man who had told him to put out into deep water and let down the nets was someone who was very close to God. He also became more conscious of his failings as a member of the chosen people. So he fell at Jesus' knees and said, 'Go away from me, Lord; I am a sinful man' (Luke 5.8).

Similarly, those who brought the adulterous woman to him were convicted by his challenge that whoever was without sin should cast the first stone at her. 'At this, those who heard began to go away one at a time, the older ones first, until only Jesus was left, with the woman still standing there' (John 8.9).

The work of the Holy Spirit both in revealing Christ and in convicting of sin is one of the themes of Christ's last discourse in the fourth gospel (John 14–16). The Father will send the Spirit on the disciples and they will know of Christ's own presence with them; he will take what is of Christ and make it known to them. But he will also convict the world of sin, because men do not believe in Christ.

Repentance, then, is our response in the Spirit when he brings us into Christ's presence. Conscious that the Lord is near us we, like Peter, become aware of our uncleanness, and we want to fall on our knees and tell him we are unworthy of him.

The Spirit may come to us in all kinds of ways. He may come when we are alone – especially when we reflect about some difficulty we are in. He may come as we read the scriptures and certain passages stir our consciences. He may come through adverse – even terrible – experiences.

Alexander Solzhenitsyn first came aware of God in the horrors of a concentration camp. There, in that unspeakable place, he had the time and inclination to listen to his own heart. Himself a Communist, he was weighed down with all he had experienced in the Communist world. He learned to listen to the inner promptings of his spirit, and the real Solzhenitsyn rose to the surface of his consciousness. In that enforced suffering and loneliness, he was raised above the mind-set of his age and environment and therefore could amazingly cry out, 'Bless you, prison, for having been in my life!' (*The Gulag Archipelago*, II, part IV, ch. 1).

But in the lives of most of us, the Spirit perhaps comes most often when we are in the presence of other Christians. I've known occasions when I've been convicted of certain sins just by being with another who has demonstrated a more mature spiritual attitude.

One such occasion was years ago just after I was ordained. As a curate in a Church of England parish in east London I did not receive a very large salary, and my stewardship of my possessions was nil. I put half-a-crown in the collection each Sunday (about a fiftieth of my weekly pay) telling myself that, since I received little from the church, I wasn't obliged to give much back.

Then I met a fellow curate from another parish, who I knew was married with two or three young children. He happened to mention in the course of conversation that he and his wife tithed their income. They gave away a tenth of all they received.

I was staggered. I knew his salary wasn't much more than mine. And I was a bachelor! I went away deeply troubled at my meanness and lack of sacrifice. The Holy Spirit was convicting me of sin through my friend's unconscious witness.

It helps to see repentance as a renewing of our conversion. Whether we made a decision for Christ at some critical moment in our lives, or whether our faith developed slowly over a number of years, reconversion is necessary because there are many times when we fall into sin. We need, as some Evangelical friends of mine say, 'to keep short accounts with God' (that is, don't let ourselves fall heavily into the debt of sinfulness).

Self-examination

When an individual turns to Christ for the first time in his life, he is conscious of certain faults which must be confessed. Sometimes one particular fault blackens his mind and he longs to be forgiven for it; sometimes it can be a cluster of minor faults which seem more serious than they really are.

But as we begin to mature in the Spirit, our ability to discern our sins increases, and we come to see other failings in ourselves which we did not notice before.

Different ages have different kinds of temptations and sins; so do different situations and lifestyles. The temptations of youth are not all the same as those of old age. The temptations of married life are not all the same as the temptations of the single life.

Our character, too, has its effect on the discernment of sin. If we are gripped in an emotional or mental disorder, our perception of what is wrong with us will also be distorted. Some people go through experiences of utter worthlessness and self-hatred in which their major problem is not repentance but self-acceptance (it is only when we accept ourselves as we are – and are able to look at ourselves more objectively – that we can begin to discern our real faults). Others lose all sense of responsibility for their actions, which means it is unrealistic to expect any repentance until their condition has been healed through counselling and prayer.

In the process of discerning, a good friend or a spiritual adviser can sometimes be a help. So can a loving marriage relationship. They help us to see ourselves as God sees us. Married life and other forms of community living can present us with unexpected and painful insights into our true selves when we see the effect we have on those close to us.

How, then, do we begin to discern what is disobedient to God in our lives?

The starting point is to hold on to the truth that we are unable to discern sin clearly without the enlightenment that comes from the Holy Spirit. Nowadays there is much interest in the gifts of the Spirit to equip God's people for service; this ought to be balanced by an equal interest in how the Spirit brings the gift of discernment to enable us to see what our sins are.

Then we need to engage in an exercise of self-examination; that is, an honest review of our lives, without trying to excuse ourselves or to pretend that we are anything other than we are.

Self-examination is never easy, though certain folk may be temperamentally more agile at it than others! Some tend to be over-scrupulous, with an excessive concern with small trifling faults which, though not grave in themselves, may have more serious underlying causes which are not recognised. Others tend to find excuses for everything that's not right in their lives, so that little sins gradually get a hold of them to separate them from God without their realising it.

When I was being prepared for confirmation at the age of nine I was instructed to make a self-examination by using a piece of paper on which were printed a long list of many possible sins. I read through the catalogue with increasing fascination, more intrigued by the sins I didn't recognise than those I knew I had committed! Lists of this kind have a limited value, though they can be helpful to those who have no idea where to begin a self-examination.

The ten commandments have been used

throughout the Christian centuries to encourage church folk to examine their consciences. They were printed in the Book of Common Prayer as a penitential preparation for communion. They were also printed in the catechism and memorised by generations of Anglicans.

An aunt of mine, who had been prepared for confirmation before the First World War, was able to recite the whole of the catechism including the ten commandments by heart. I used to test her sometimes by asking one of the questions at random and listen to her as she reeled off the appropriate answer. Checking what she said with the catechism, I always found her word perfect.

Though reflecting a different society from our own, the section in the catechism on the ten commandments overviews Christian discipleship with pragmatic directness:

Catechist: What dost thou chiefly learn by these commandments?

Answer: I learn two things: my duty towards God, and my duty towards my neighbour.

Catechist: What is thy duty towards God?

Answer: My duty towards God is to believe in him, to fear him, and to love him, with all my heart, with all my mind, with all my soul, and with all my strength; to worship him, to give him thanks, to put my whole trust in him, to call upon him, to honour his holy Name and his Word, and to serve him truly all the days of my life.

Catechist: What is thy duty towards thy neighbour?

Answer: My duty towards my neighbour is to

love him as myself, and to do to all men as I would they should do unto me: to love, honour, and succour my father and mother: to honour and obey the Queen, and all that are put in authority under her: to submit myself to all my governors, teachers, spiritual pastors and masters: to order myself lowly and reverently to all my betters: to hurt nobody by word nor deed: to be true and just in all my dealing: to bear no malice or hatred in my heart: to keep my hands from picking and stealing, and my tongue from evil-speaking, lying, and slandering: to keep my body in temperance, soberness, and chastity: not to covet nor desire other men's goods; but to learn and labour truly to get mine own living, and to do my duty in that state of life, unto which it shall please God to call me.

My aunt – and the millions of other Anglican children who were brought up to memorise these passages – at least had guidelines about the rightness and wrongness of things. Their consciences were partially formed by the exercise.

The weakness with this kind of self-examination is that it sees Christian conduct in terms of keeping laws rather in terms of maintaining our relationship with God. It tells us what not to do rather than what we should be capable of in the power of the Spirit as children of God.

If we think of sin more as a breaking of relationships rather than as a breaking of laws, then we are more likely to look to Jesus as our model rather than to the commandments as a checklist. I'm sure the checklist is necessary from time to time; but only as a guide to our new life in the new covenant of God.

Pictures in an Exhibition

The beatitudes (Matthew 5.3–10) provide us with one way of looking at the character of Jesus as a model against which we can measure our own lives. We become more aware of our failings as we come closer to him; so these sayings about those who are 'blessed' present us with a mirror in which we see ourselves more clearly as we really are.

For example, we can imagine that each beatitude is a painting of Christ based on a different aspect of his character. The paintings are exhibited on the walls of a long gallery, and we are strolling slowly along from one to the next, pausing at each one for a few moments to reflect on what the picture tells us about Jesus and realising how we, by contrast, fall short of his example.

Blessed are the poor in spirit, for theirs is the kingdom of heaven

Humility is the foundation of Christian discipleship, for by it we turn away from ourselves and our self-sufficiency to live in complete dependence on God.

The humility of Christ, expressed in his obedience to the Father in becoming man, was demonstrated powerfully in the events leading to the crucifixion – the trial, the scourging, the carrying of the cross, and the submission to the nailing, the agony, and the death.

A humble person does not esteem or praise himself; he has no self-complacency; he knows his true worth. His head is not turned when others admire him, for he knows his gifts and abilities come only from God. He is honest through and through. He does not talk about himself or his family to his own advantage; he has no sense of superiority; he does not despise those who seem to be less able than he is.

When others are critical of him, or sarcastic, he does not react or become resentful; when they neglect him or humiliate him, he rejects all ideas of revenge. Rather, he is thankful that through such experiences he can draw closer to his Lord, who was also rejected by men. He learns how to forgive. He forgets himself for the love of God, and already he has begun to taste the joys of eternal life. 'I have been crucified with Christ and I no longer live, but Christ lives in me' (Galatians 2.20).

Blessed are those who mourn, for they will be comforted

Through the ministry of Jesus we catch glimpses of his mourning for the state of mankind. His detestation of Satan, his compassion for sinners, his weeping over Jerusalem – these events and others reveal a deep sadness at the predicament of fallen humanity.

The disciple of Christ mourns his own deficiencies. Within him there is a sense of contrition for his sins – not in morbid introspection, but in a frank acknowledgement that he is always dependent on the mercy of God.

And, like Jesus, he mourns also for the sorrows and tragedies he sees around him. He, too, is a man of compassion – suffering with others who suffer. He cares for the tragedies in the world, as well as for neighbours who are involved in life's pains and disappointments – sickness, accidents, unemployment, assaults, and the death of loved ones.

And the more he experiences this Christ-like compassion, the more he wants to express to God his sorrow for the sin and evil which cause much suffering in the world. He also wants to act to remedy unjust and painful situations where he can.

Blessed are the meek, for they will inherit the earth

This beatitude is taken from Psalm 37.11, which says the meek will not only inherit the land but will 'enjoy great peace'. Meekness is often misunderstood. It doesn't mean that we are to let others do what they like with us. Jesus was meek – but he was also a man of great power and self-control, through total openness to the Holy Spirit.

The meek disciple knows where his weaknesses are – giving way to destructive emotions, unloving thoughts, immoral desires. His meekness prompts him to invite the Spirit to take control of his life and enables him to submit to his rule.

Then he experiences an inward harmony which has a calming influence on others, a clarifying vision, and a true judgement. He is submissive to the will of God in all circumstances of his daily life, and in his relations with others.

All kinds of things try us: the weather, our infirmities or disabilities, misunderstandings by others, our family responsibilities, uncongenial times at work, our friend's moods, the insinuations of those who don't like us, our relations and their apparent lack of concern for us. Christ suffered all these, and never once did he complain or show distaste or boredom. The meek person reflects the same peace as he seeks God's will and enters into the true possession of all that God gives him.

Blessed are those who hunger and thirst for righteousness, for they will be filled

'I have come down from heaven not to do my will but to do the will of him who sent me' (John 6.38).

We are called to have the same foundation for our lives as our Saviour: to have the highest ideals, to aim at perfection, and to do God's will with all the strength God pours on us in Christ through his Holy Spirit.

We must therefore be prepared to suffer privation in worldly things in order to be filled with all that God wants to give us. And desire for God and love of him, and therefore of our neighbour, must be the decisive and controlling motive of our lives.

Blessed are the merciful, for they will be shown mercy

Jesus must have been sorely tried at times by the people who filled his daily life, by their stupidity, their dullness, their cruelty, their refusal to respond to what was obvious to him – his Father's love. Yet he only withdrew himself from them in order to pray, and he never refused them sympathy and help. The Gospel tells us of three years of ceaseless giving-out, of continual contact with fellow human beings, of self-sacrificing mercy, yet all the time he knew what was in man and what lay in store for him (John 2.25).

In Jesus we see the great demonstration of the mercy of God – the mercy we are to reflect in our dealings with others. It is easy to be critical of people, of their standards, of their families, of their attainments, of their interests, and of the way they spend their time and money. We all have within us an eager capacity to be judgemental of our neighbours for their faults and mistakes.

But a compassionate heart, touched by the mercy of God, is generous towards others – generous to the point of excess. Our Lord could forgive his murderers, excusing their deed because he understood them completely. Because God is merciful, he sent his Son to be our Saviour: thus underlying God's mercy is God's love. To test ourselves against the love of God we only have to read slowly the hymn to love in 1 Corinthians 13.

Blessed are the pure in heart, for they will see God

One of the great biblical descriptions of God is that he is the God of light, and his light appeared in the life of Jesus. So our Lord said of himself, 'I am the light of the world. Whoever follows me will never walk in darkness, but will have the light of life' (John 8.12). The faithful disciple shares in this light of Christ, which enlightens him inwardly and outwardly.

He is enlightened inwardly because his heart is illuminated by God: 'God who said, "Let light shine out of darkness", made his light shine in our hearts to give us the light of the knowledge of the glory of God in the face of Christ' (2 Corinthians 4.6). And he is enlightened outwardly in that his attitude and conduct, and particularly his relationships with others, reflect the light of God: 'Whoever loves his brother lives in the light' (1 John 2.10).

The disciple with a pure heart is one with eyes only for the things of God. That does not mean he is one with his head in the clouds, taking no notice of what goes on around him; nor does it mean that he shuts himself off from everyday affairs. But being in the world he is not of it; and while using the things of the world, he sees them not primarily for his own enjoyment but as a ladder towards God and as a means of glorifying him.

Purity of heart results in seeing all things within the purpose for which God has made them. That means the right use of our bodies and minds; it means submitting our emotions and intentions to the purifying grace of God.

It also results in seeing people as men and women made in the image of God and created to fulfil his purposes – ultimately as his disciples and worshippers. So individuals are not statistics or sex-objects or slaves. They are God's children – potentially, if they are not yet believers; actually, if they have accepted their Saviour.

Blessed are the peacemakers, for they will be called sons of God

Jesus brought the peace of God to those who came to him in their needs and who followed him when he called them. But that peace is not found in the absence of human strife: the prevalence of sin makes such harmony impossible until evil is defeated on the last day. The peace Jesus brought is the peace of his indwelling presence in our lives. 'Peace I leave with you; my peace I give you. I do not give to you as the world gives' (John 14.27).

The peacemaker is one who has been gifted by the Holy Spirit with the authority of Christ to bring peace into the affairs of those around him. The man who is at peace with himself is one who, having renewed his repentance, offers himself afresh each day to God; from this follows a peacefulness in his relationships with his neighbours.

Blessed are those who are persecuted because of righteousness, for theirs is the kingdom of heaven

Righteousness and justice are two English words for one word in the Bible. In our language righteousness is almost a simile for personal holiness, while justice has more to do with right relationships and fair dealings with others. But all are embraced within the biblical view of God's righteousness.

The holiness of Jesus shines through every word and act in the gospels; so does the rightness and fairness of his relationships with others. And, because he was persecuted literally to death for such righteousness, his kingdom is open to all those who stand on the side of God's righteousness.

To take such stands may involve us in opposing what is conventional in the world. The person who does this can be accused of being unreasonable, puritanical or even unloving. He may well become unpopular, especially if he has to oppose the attitudes and intentions of individuals in his own family, and the cost may be great. It is the fear of this which often leads people to compromise God's law.

Because God's righteousness includes justice for others, particularly the poor, underprivileged and the oppressed, the righteous person finds himself alongside those who struggle for justice in the social, political and economic affairs of the world, where such a struggle is necessary.

He also sometimes finds himself with strange allies. Having invited the churches of Manchester to march through the city in the cause of racial equality some years ago, I was startled to discover that the friendly man walking beside me in the road was the secretary of the local Communist party!

But there is every possible difference between one who engages in that struggle to satisfy an angry, inner neurosis, and one who engages in it in obedience to the leading of the Prince of Peace. It is faith in God above all else which enables him to keep this inner stillness. 'You will keep in perfect peace him whose mind is steadfast, because he trusts in you' (Isaiah 26.3).

Contrition and Amendment

So we conclude our tour round the picture gallery, and as the character of Christ is revealed through our minds and imaginations, we become more aware of how our own lives differ from his. Within us we will be aware of two emotions.

One is a feeling of contrition. When we look at Jesus Christ, and particularly at the culmination of his sacrifice on the cross, we sense within ourselves a brokenness, a realisation that we have fallen so far short of what God intends us to be and that we are in our sinfulness offensive to his goodness and holiness.

Contrition comes when we understand how our disobedience wounds the heart of Jesus Christ, and we hear him say, 'My people, what have I done to you?' (Micah 6.3). It is an attitude of love towards God which acknowledges our worthlessness: 'The sacrifices of God are a broken spirit; a broken and contrite heart, O God, you will not despise' (Psalm 51.17).

The second emotion will be a longing for forgiveness so that at least we have a new beginning from which to resume our pilgrimage with Jesus again. With the psalmist we say, 'My soul thirsts for God, for the living God . . . Put your hope in God, for I will yet praise him, my Saviour and my God' (Psalm 42.2, 11).

With the contrition and the longing for forgiveness comes a determination to amend our lives and to avoid sin in the future. Without such an act of will, our repentance is incomplete.

To sum up: self-examination is not an end in itself; it is only valid in so far as it assists us to grow in union with God and to become more Christ-like. Contrition and an impulse to amend our lives are

the fruits of repentance which inspire us to confess
our sins – the next stage for entering into the glorious
liberty of the children of God.

For Discussion

(1) What factors in modern society make it difficult
for us to make a realistic self-examination?
(2) How often do we need to make the kind of self-
examination suggested in this chapter?

Bible Reading

1 John 1.1–10

verses 1–4   Compare the introduction to this letter
with the introduction to the gospel
of John 1.1–4. *Heard . . .' seen . . .,
looked at . . ., touched. . .*: affirming
the humanity of Christ. *We proclaim
to you the eternal life*: Christ, because
he is the living one and he is the
source of life.

    5–7   *Light . . . darkness*: good/evil; true/
false.

  8–10   *Faithful and just*: God will respond to
those who confess their sins because
he promises to forgive (Jeremiah
31.34; Micah 7.18–20) and it is
impossible for him to contradict his
word.

5

Confession

Confessing our guilt is what is called an archetypal experience – that is to say, something so deeply anchored in the very structure of our human psyche that the need for it will never disappear. We will all, at some time or other, experience an irrepressible urge to tell others some – if not all – of the things we've done wrong.

When an individual discovers a need to confess, there may be different motives.

(1) There is the need which an ordinary, normal individual has to unburden himself or herself and thus create a better set of social conditions for improved relationships with his or her family, friends and others. That is a social and psychological task.

A police officer dealing with young people who have broken the law told me that, when given an opportunity, they frequently confess to everything they have ever done in their lives, and much else besides.

'I get the impression no one's ever sat down and listened to them before,' he said. 'They seem so grateful they can get it off their chests.'

He added that, once he had heard their stories, he did all he could to avoid charging them.

(2) There is the need which neurotics have to talk about their thoughts, feelings and deeds – many of

them evil – to a significant person in their lives in order to recover their sense of balance and their personal integrity. That is a therapeutic task.

As I've just said, making an individual confession of personal faults is a complex psychological action. If we do it before professional counsellors, we are laying ourselves open to them for their help and advice. The counsellor takes notes of all that we say about ourselves and, from the resources of his or her training and experience, leads us to the point where we can understand ourselves and maybe accept ourselves more as the person we are.

Although the effect may be beneficial – indeed, it may be quite a healing exercise – it remains at a psychological level. It need not have any spiritual dimension whatever (though it could have, under the guidance of the right kind of counsellor).

(3) There is the need which Christians have for their sins to be forgiven. That is a moral–spiritual task, and it must be dealt with as such by recognising them as penitents and encouraging them to make their confession to God in an appropriate manner.

When we confess our sins to God, a new dimension is introduced. We are making that confession because we believe he is a merciful and righteous Father, who has opened a new and living way for us to approach him through Jesus Christ. As we have seen in previous chapters, a vital element in that approach is that we should allow his Spirit to show us our need for forgiveness, and then in faith look to the Father for the forgiveness which has been won for us by his Son on the cross.

The confession which we, as Christians, make of our sins, therefore, is not made for psychological purposes, though these may be involved with it.

70

There are neurotic elements in the makeup of all of us and we must not imagine that we are immune from them. But our primary intention is to confess our sins to God.

And we do this because confession is a necessary preliminary in our approach to God in prayer – the recitation of our sins being a sign of our repentance and of our desire for his forgiveness.

We say to him: 'Look, Lord, this is how I see myself as I am instructed by your Word and illuminated by your Holy Spirit: I recognise in myself the following disobediences and weaknesses. . .'

The fact that often we don't know what to say, or that we always seem to have to admit to the same sins is not necessarily a sign of shallowness or lack of self-knowledge. It may equally be an expression of deep sincerity and a realisation of human complexity. The more we become aware of our sinfulness in the light of the Holy Spirit, the more we also become aware of the inextricable mixing within us of the tares and the wheat growing together until the final harvest.

We discern the labyrinthine alleyways of evil within ourselves, the compromises we make through cowardice, our conniving acquiescence in that which leads to sin, our inner disorder, our refusals to commit ourselves, our pretexts for sloth, our running away from God and our attempts to buy back his favour, and our lack of generosity and our unloving attitudes towards our neighbour.

Well, so be it. If we are honestly trying to own up to God all that we believe is wrong with ourselves in his eyes, then we must trust he understands the reasons for our blindness – for not seeing all of the beam in our own eye.

The list of sins which we present to God is only a sign, an offering of our repentance and contrition.

No oblation we can make will ever be perfect. But God meets us where we are – or, rather, at that point in our Christian pilgrimage we have reached when we make our confession.

'While he was still a long way off, his father saw him and was filled with compassion for him; he ran to his son, threw his arms around him, and kissed him' (Luke 15.20).

The father in Jesus' parable did not wait for the lost son to reach him and confess his sin before he embraced him; he rushed out to meet him and expressed his love before the first words of his son's confession were uttered.

Two Sides of a Confession

When we study the use of the word 'confession' we find it has a twofold connotation. It can refer to a confession of faith, and it can also refer to a confession of sin.

To confess our faith means to declare publicly a personal relationship with and allegiance to God. When we do this we make an act of open and joyful commitment to God in the presence of others, binding ourselves loyally to him.

In the Old Testament such a confession of faith frequently has the character of praise, where the believer in gratitude declares what God has done either for Israel or for himself as God's servant. It is made in the context of the covenant which God has established with his people.

Thus thanksgiving and praise are often closely associated with confession of sin, because God is thanked and praised for his mighty acts of mercy and deliverance. A good example of this is Psalm 32, where the psalmist acknowledges his guilt and then summons the congregation to praise God for his mercy and righteousness:

> I said, 'I will confess
>   my transgressions to the Lord' –
> and you forgave
>   the guilt of my sin. . .
> Rejoice in the Lord and be glad, you righteous;
>   sing, all you who are upright in heart!
>   (Psalm 32.5,11)

In the New Testament 'to confess' is generally used with reference to faith in Christ. It means to acknowledge, to admit, to declare that something is so. In this sense that Paul wrote that 'every tongue [should] confess that Jesus Christ is Lord, to the glory of God the Father' (Philippians 2.11). 'If you confess with your mouth, "Jesus is Lord", and believe in your heart that God raised him from the dead, you will be saved' (Romans 10.9).

'To confess Christ' gathers up all the Old Testament aspects of thanksgiving and praise, as well as of willing submission. It means, however, more than a mental assent; it means we pledge ourselves in loyalty to Jesus Christ and acknowledge him as Messiah (Mark 4.29), as the Son of God (Matthew 8.29), as he who came in the flesh (1 John 4.2), and as our risen and ascended Lord (Romans 10.9).

Formally we confess our faith together when we recite the creed in worship. The Christian creeds developed out of the need to question the catechumens who presented themselves for baptism to ascertain whether or not they believed in God as their creator, Jesus Christ as their Saviour, and the Holy Spirit as the one who leads them into obedience and holiness. The texts of the creeds were elaborated when it became necessary to guard against heretical teachings. When we stand and say the creed we are reaffirming the faith in which we were baptised into the Christian fellowship.

This leads to a confession of our sins. To confess Christ is to confess that he 'died for our sins'; conversely to confess our sins is to acknowledge our true condition and look to him for forgiveness (1 John 1.5–10).

Confession of faith and confession of sins, then, are two sides of the same coin. It is because we confess our faith in Jesus Christ as our Lord and Saviour that we recognise the need to confess our sins in repentance and ask for forgiveness; and it is because of that same faith we are assured of God's forgiveness through him.

Both confession of sins and confession of faith in Jesus Christ are works of the Holy Spirit. The Spirit who convicts us of our guilt, making us realise the need to confess our sins (John 16.8), is the same Spirit who enables us to affirm with our hearts as well as our minds that Jesus Christ is Lord (1 Corinthians 12.3).

Although addressed to God, confession of faith in Jesus Christ is made openly 'before men' (Matthew 10.32). Christ Jesus made 'the good confession' while testifying before Pontius Pilate, and Timothy also made a 'good confession in the presence of many witnesses' (1 Timothy 6.12–13). The very nature of confessing faith in Jesus Christ implies doing it publicly. It may be a costly exercise.

Confession of sin is similarly addressed to God, but it may also be made before men, either in a corporate confession made generally by a congregation or individually before others. The epistle of James includes an injunction to Christians to confess their sins to one another. It is given as part of the ministry to the sick, where the elders are to anoint the sick and to pray over them (James 5.16). True repentance may require acknowledgement of guilt before a brother (Matthew 5.23–24). It, too, may be costly.

Our confessions of faith and confessions of sin are signs that the old man in us is dying with Christ and that we are becoming the Lord's own possession. In making these confessions we are being called to participate through the Holy Spirit in the vicarious intercession of Christ, 'the apostle and high priest whom we confess' (Hebrews 3.1), who has already 'confessed' our sins on the cross and given praise to God.

Christ will one day confess before the Father those who confess him today, and deny those who deny him (Matthew 10.32–33). Our confessions are a fore-shadowing of the confession of all God's people on the last day, when every tongue will confess that Jesus Christ is Lord (Romans 14.11–12).

Private and General Confessions

When we confess our sins to God, we tell him we are sorry for the things we have thought, said and done which we know were disobedient to his law. We own up before him to all the sins we have delib-erately committed, the sins we committed impul-sively, and the sins we have committed which we have not discerned. We also confess our fault in not doing what we should have done.

Even if we are not feeling particularly sorry, we still make such a prayer as an act of obedience. It is not feelings which make prayers real; it is the inten-tion to reject sin and to amend our lives.

Very often this exercise will seem almost mechan-ical, and we shall be tempted to neglect it on the grounds that we are being hypocritical. But a discipline – the basic meaning of that word is 'being a disciple' – usually entails setting aside what Paul called the 'flesh' and yielding to the Spirit. The devil tries to convince us that a confession of sin is unnecessary, or unreal, or inadequate: this is the strategy of the evil one when we try to draw near to God through penitence and humility.

Before we go to bed at night is the obvious time to make such a confession. It is a wise family that sorts out its disagreements and hurts at the end of the day: 'Do not let the sun go down while you are still angry' (Ephesians 4.29). The same principle applies in our relationships with God. The grace and mercy of God comes new every morning if we have confessed our sins to him the night before.

We look back over the events of the day and mentally tick off our disobediences and omissions. In our imagination they are filthy articles of clothing which we take off and throw into the fire of Christ's sacrifice. With each imaginary gesture we say, 'Lord have mercy'. We don't have to spend a lot of time confessing what we've done or not done, but we try to be as thorough as we can.

On some days there may not be much that we can discern or remember. It's been a busy day, or an ordinary day, without much opportunity for deliberate acts of disobedience to God. But we still offer God a prayer of confession because we know that at no time are we perfect in our lives.

Church services provide us with an opportunity to join with others in making corporate acts of penitence. General confessions enable us to confess our sinfulness together just as creeds enable us to confess our faith together. In modern liturgical rites general confessions are often accompanied by periods of silence for recollection.

'Let us call to mind our sins,' says the worship leader.

Kneeling or sitting with the rest of the congregation, we briefly review the past week. We reaffirm our penitence for the sins we have already confessed in our daily prayers. We make a note of anything we need to put right – apologising to someone we have offended, fulfilling something we've not done. We also join in the penitence of the congregation for its corporate failures. We think of our share in the sins of the church in our day – the weakness of its witness to the Gospel of the kingdom, the half-heartedness of its opposition to the social ills in our world, the shame of its complacency in the midst of Christian disunity.

Then we can make our own the words of the general confession as we recite them in chorus with the rest:

Father eternal, giver of light and grace,

We've just seen that light is the biblical attribute which manifests God's holiness, and that light is reflected in the lives of those who are obedient to him. Grace is the word for God's favour, his mercy and his loving-kindness, the gift we sinners need if we are to be accepted again by him.

we have sinned against you and against our fellow men,

Our disobediences have a vertical dimension – against God – and a horizontal one – against our fellow believers.

in what we have thought,
in what we have said and done,

Sin affects the working of our minds, hearts and

spirits; it shows itself in our words and in our activities.

through ignorance, through weakness,
through our own deliberate fault.

The three grades of sin are for our benefit. They are not excuses for our wrongdoing ('It was only a little sin!'). All sin is sin; but the circumstances in which we are tempted and fall into sin differ, and the differences are recognised here.

We have wounded your love,
and marred your image in us.

The 'wound of love' is a traditional image in Christian spirituality for the cross: there Christ was 'wounded for our transgressions'. At times there has been a special devotion among some Christians to the wounds of Christ on the cross as marks of salvation. We are made in the image of God, and sin obscures that image.

We are sorry and ashamed,
and repent of all our sins.

Sorrow and shame are the ingredients which make up contrition.

For the sake of your Son Jesus Christ, who died
*   for us,*
forgive us all that is past;

It is no accident that at the heart of the Christian Gospel stands the cross. We can highlight other aspects of our message and experience as much as we want, but the saving fact is the cross. What the Father has done in the death of the Son contains the most profound answer to the needs of man.

and lead us out of darkness
to walk as children of light. Amen.

The prayer ends by giving us an opportunity to tell God that we wish to amend our lives and to set sin behind us. Walking in the light is the Johannine image of faithful discipleship.

Before the Cross

The act of confessing our sins brings us in spirit to the foot of the cross. It was for these that he died – my self-centredness, my lack of love, my greed, my ambition, my immorality, my anger . . .

And as we contemplate the cross, those three concepts or themes of the mystery of the atonement which I outlined in Chapter 2 become more than studies in biblical theology. They are revelations of the love of God in Jesus Christ which reach out to meet us according to our spiritual and psychological needs in our confession of sin. Let us take each one in turn and see how it might bring a deeper awareness of the forgiveness which flows from the cross for different personalities.

(1) Perhaps I'm the kind of person who finds it difficult to accept responsibility for my sin. I tell myself that I think and act in the way I do because that's how I was brought up to behave, or because the circumstances within which I find myself cause me to react in that manner. We all have built-in mechanisms for excusing the unacceptable sides of our character when we glimpse our own failings.

But when I look at the cross and see there what my sins did to the Son of Man, then I begin to recognise the horror of what I'm confessing. That is what my failings mean in terms of God's love for me. That is what they cost the Servant of God as a vicarious act on my behalf.

Julian of Norwich's *Revelations of Divine Love* are often reprinted in collections of devotional classics, indicating that modern Christians still find in them a guide to contemplating the meaning of the cross. This fourteenth-century English mystic asked God in her prayers to be allowed to have a vision of Christ in his Passion in order that she might gain a better understanding of it, and this unusual request was granted to Julian during a severe illness in her thirty-first year when she thought she was dying.

Between 4 o'clock and 9 o'clock on the morning of 8 May 1373 she received a series of fifteen visions, with a sixteenth the next evening, of Christ on the cross, and her book is a prolonged meditation on those visions which she wrote years later. In the last paragraphs she concluded:

> From the time [these visions were] first revealed to me I often longed to know what our Lord meant. More than fifteen years later I was answered. Spiritual enlightenment came with the words, 'Do you want to know what our Lord meant in all this? Learn it well: love was what he meant. Who showed it to you? Love. What did he show you? Love. Why did he show it? Out of love. Stay with this and you will learn and know more about love.'
>
> (ch. 86)

(2) Perhaps I'm the kind of person who is burdened with a weighty sense of guilt, and making my confession painfully revives my guilt complex and sense of worthlessness. Assuming that I have begun to accept this characteristic about myself, after counselling and inner healing, then the

resurgence of that complex will draw me to the cross as the sign of the sin-offering which Christ made on my behalf.

The substitutionary theory of the atonement is rather played down by theologians these days. They prefer to teach that Jesus is the representative of sinful and suffering humanity. The cross 'represents' the way in which God is one with us in all that we have to accept in this world, including death itself.

But it is difficult to see how a representative can be anything other than a substitute if that representative shares in our humanity. Indeed, Jesus is more than that, for he was not elected or chosen by us (as most representatives are) but he was sent by God to be totally one with us in our predicament.

Jesus is my substitute because he takes my sin, complex, grief, despair and suffering and he carries the burden of them for me. He enters so deeply into my situation and that of mankind that we are made free of all that overwhelms us through the gift of his death.

I can, then, ask him to lift my burden of guilt as I confess my sins, knowing that he has already accepted it on the cross. The scapegoat was sent running away into the desert, ritually bearing the sins of the people; so Christ in reality bears my sins and takes them away through his sacrifice.

(3) Perhaps I'm the kind of person who feels trapped in my sinfulness. As I make my confession and tell God yet again the all-too-familiar list of transgressions (do I need to do this every time if he knows them already?) I feel as if I am marking out the walls of the prison.

Christian spirituality teaches that there is a fine balance between affirming that we are already saved in Jesus Christ and recognising that we are still on the way to salvation. This is illustrated when we put various New Testament texts side by side. For example, Paul can write in Ephesians 2.8, 'It is by grace that you have been saved, through faith – and this is not from yourselves, it is the gift of God.' But he can also write in 1 Corinthians 1.18, 'The message of the cross is foolishness to those who are perishing, but to us who are being saved it is the power of God.'

Calvary was a historic event at a certain date in history (the earlier Christian creeds emphasised this by stating that Christ suffered 'under Pontius Pilate', meaning during the years that Pilate was Roman procurator or governor of Judaea, AD 26/27 to 36/37 – the precise dates are uncertain). In that sense the victory has already been won for us and we have entered into that redemption.

But it is also true that we still have to accept that redeeming work for ourselves day by day so that the victory of the cross becomes a reality in our lives now.

If we feel trapped in our sins, then, as we make our confession, we can look at the cross as a sign that the prison walls have already been flattened around us like the walls of Jericho. What we are confessing is not just our wretchedness but also our joy in being delivered by Christ. The cross then truly becomes for us 'the power of God'.

The story of the Passion in the fourth gospel is particularly relevant for us. These twenty-four hours of Jesus' earthly life are portrayed by John as a victory procession. During the cross-examination before Pilate it is Christ who is in control of the proceedings and Pilate who is the confused seeker: 'What is truth?' (John 18.38). On the road to Calvary Jesus carries his own cross without any assistance from Simon of Cyrene (19.17). Nothing whatever will make Pilate alter the title which he caused to be written above the crucified man, 'Jesus of Nazareth, the King of the Jews' (19.19). And the final cry from the cross is a great shout of triumph. 'It is finished' (19.30). God has indeed reigned from the tree.

Whatever our need, then, the scriptures bring out for us different aspects of God's forgiving love in Christ for our spiritual comfort and renewal. They show us that the cross not only takes away from us the guilt which our sin causes but also conquers the enemy who puts the temptation to sin in our path. In the words of A. M. Toplady's hymn:

> Let the water and the blood,
>> From thy riven side which flowed,
> Be of sin the double cure:
>> Cleanse me from its guilt and power.

Confession to Others

Confession of our sins to God may involve us in confessing to others as well. This is obviously necessary if we have wronged them in any way. But for the reasons discussed in the previous chapters, there is also a place for a confession of our sins to one another in order that the Christian fellowship may be cleansed and strengthened.

Indeed, such a discipline is enjoyed in James 5.15–16, in the context of prayer for and anointing of the sick by the elders of the church: 'The prayer offered in faith will make the sick person well; the Lord will raise him up. If he had sinned, he will be forgiven. Therefore confess your sins to each other and pray for each other so that you may be healed.'

83

Confession of sins has been part of the church's ministry to the sick from the beginning; but healing in its wider connotation involves the spiritual health of the Christian fellowship as well. Once sins have been confessed to one another and forgiveness offered, then the church is in a better state of spiritual fitness for her mission.

That is why the confession of sins has been the spiritual springboard for movements of renewal. The East African revival in the 1930s began when white Christians began to ask forgiveness from their black companions for the attitudes of racism which they had adopted towards them.

In the diary which he kept of the East African revival, and later published under the title, *Quest for the Highest* (1981), J. E. Church transcribed a note he had made in 1934:

> What became the great fruit of the revival [was] deep oneness and fellowship with the Africans. We found that when once we had repented and in some cases asked forgiveness for our prejudice and white superiority, a new realm in relationships was entered into which altered the character of all our work. (p. 99)

The same was true in relationships between blacks. Blasio Kigori, an African teacher at a school in Gahini, wrote in 8 August 1935 how the trouble certain boys had caused him made him look again at his own life. He renewed his renunciation of sin, received baptism in the Spirit, and prayed earnestly for the students under his charge:

> 'The whole atmosphere of the term has absolutely changed. Three boys came to me and openly confessed their sins. The movement went on gradually, and now there are nearly a dozen or

more than that who have been born again. These have changed the whole tone of the school. Nowadays they come to me as their friend, and consult me in their trouble. It is a joy that I have never experienced since the time I first began to work for Christ.' (p. 112)

In missionaries' conferences and other gatherings there was stress on 'the second experience of the cross'. They took John Bunyan's *Pilgrim's Progress* and pointed out that it was when Christian lost his burden that his heart became 'glad and lightsome', and that this deeper experience of the blood of Jesus results in the finding of the 'rest for the people of God' (Hebrews 4.9) – rest from guilt and work.

J. E. Church commented:

Humanity has a poor vocabulary to express the deepest experiences of the spirit, especially this emancipating and renewing vision of the meaning of the cross, and the perhaps inadequate expression 'being broken' began to be used to describe the 'broken and contrite heart' of Psalm 51. Thus brokenness has become a heartfelt prayer request in testimonies throughout East Africa. (p. 157)

But how can we do this kind of thing today? What is available for us when we have prayed – even begged God – for forgiveness, but have sensed no release? What hope is there for us when we have made a self-examination and spent time alone with the Lord, telling him we are repentant, but doubted whether he has been listening? What assurance can we have that, 'If we confess our sins, he is faithful and just and will forgive us our sins and purify us from all unrighteousness' (1 John 1.9)?

We will discuss this problem in the next chapter.

For Discussion

(1) What are the advantages and disadvantages of using a set formula like the one in this chapter for making one's confession?

(2) Can we totally ignore our feelings in deciding whether or not to make a confession?

Bible Reading

Luke 15.11–32

verses 11–16 The father was exceptionally generous in giving the younger son his portion of the inheritance. The rabbis advised against it. Looking after pigs was the ultimate indignity for a Jew.

17–20 The experience of repentance.

21–24 Signs of distinction: *long robe* for an honoured person; *ring* for authority; *sandals* for a son (slaves went barefoot); *fattened calf* for a special occasion.

28–32 While the attitude of the father reflects the mercy of God, the complaint of the elder son reflects the reaction of humanity. *This son of yours*: he would not even recognise him as his brother. *Everything I have is yours*: the father's love is as great for both his sons.

6

Absolution

In times of spiritual renewal, like the East African revival, Christians have been moved to make open confessions of their sins before their brothers and sisters in worship. While there may be occasions when such confessions are appropriate, it is not a practice to be encouraged. The Holy Spirit may move individuals in groups and congregations to acknowledge specific faults before one another, but the pastoral leadership must be sure that these initiatives come from God and not from any other (exhibitionist?) spirit. The lesson of Christian history is that open confessions are easily liable to abuse and the overall effects far from edifying for the church.

Some religious orders have a form of mutual confession in what is known as 'a chapter of faults', when the community meets and each member confesses if he or she has broken the community's rules during the past week. It is only in such close, family-like groups that the practice can be handled discreetly.

In the eastern churches it has been customary for Christians to confess their sins privately to a member of a religious order, who is more likely to be lay than ordained, or to someone who is known to be a holy and wise disciple of the Lord. But in the west private confessions have been made almost exclusively to a priest or an ordained minister, who is bound by the discipline of the church to maintain strict confidentiality (the seal of the confessional).

The idea of confessing one's sins to a priest is not as controversial now as it was a few generations ago. When the practice was revived in the Church of England in the latter half of the nineteenth century, it provoked a dispute that rumbled on to the middle of the twentieth. The Anglo-Catholics were primarily responsible for the revival of the practice, for their aim was to restore sacramental worship and traditional discipline to the life of the Anglican Communion. They believed that the sacrament of penance, as it was called, was a necessary part of this.

A leading advocate was Dr E. B. Pusey, who in 1878 published an English translation of Abbé Gaume's *Manual for Confessors*. This book gave detailed directions on how to deal with all kinds of human weaknesses, and a long preface written by Pusey defended the practice of confessing sins to a priest in the light of the Church of England's formularies and history. It was welcomed by the increasing number of clergy who were hearing confessions in parishes, on missions, and in religious houses, and who were discovering that the assurance of God's forgiveness that they were able to pronounce encouraged many to greater faithfulness and holiness.

But pamphlets and books were pouring from the presses on either side of the debate. For the Revd T. T. Carter, Rector of Clewer, the confessional was essential for 'winning and guiding souls to God' (1869). For the Revd A. R. Buckland 'the history of the confessional was the foulest blot in the record of the Church' (1901). Echoes of the controversy reached the popular press from time to time, so that most Englishmen were left with the satisfying prejudice that confession was a Romish practice from which they had been delivered by the Protestant Reformation.

Going to confession has never been as widespread among Anglicans as it was among Roman Catholics. Only a tiny minority of Anglicans made their confessions regularly, although many more did so at critical moments in their lives, such as before their confirmation or when they were troubled by a serious sin. Once the controversy died away, it gradually ceased to be a distinctly Anglo-Catholic practice. The retreat before my ordination in 1953 was led by an Evangelical vicar who was regarded as being one of the best confessors in Oxford.

To understand the practice of confessing sins to a priest, we have to dip into the long history of how the discipline has been exercised in the centuries since the close of the New Testament era down to our own times. It is a complex story, with many related topics – penitential exercises and indulgences, theological debates about the nature of the priest's authority to absolve sins, spiritual direction and ethical questions, canon law and the seal of the confessional, and so on. Here I will only touch on a few examples from the past.

We have already seen how from New Testament times the church barred from her fellowship those who had committed grievous sins after their baptism and then readmitted them to the community once they had repented.

In the early centuries the sign of reconciliation was not the prayer pronounced by the bishop but the receiving of the eucharist. Joining in the worship of your Christian community and sharing with them in the bread and the wine of the sacrament was the outward sign that your sins were forgiven.

Dionysius, Bishop of Alexandria (died about AD 264), told a story which illustrates this.

There was once an old man called Serapion who lived a blameless life as a Christian for many years. But at a time when one of the periodic persecutions of the church swept over the Roman Empire, he lost his courage and offered a sacrifice to the gods – in other words, he apostasised. Later, he bitterly repented of his unfaithfulness and often prayed to be reconciled, but he was refused.

When he fell ill and was dying, he was unconscious for three days, but on the fourth day he rallied and calling his grandson to him, said, 'How long, child, are you all determined to keep me alive? Do please hurry, and let me go quickly! You go yourself, and bring me one of the presbyters.'

The boy ran to fetch the presbyter, but found him ill and not able to leave his bed. But the presbyter sent with the boy a small portion of the eucharistic bread, telling him to soak it in water and let it fall into the old man's mouth.

Serapion revived when his grandson returned home long enough to receive the sacrament from him; and then he died. Dionysius commented, 'Was he not plainly preserved and kept alive until he was released and, his sin blotted out, could be honoured for his many good deeds?' (Eusebius, *The History of the Church*, vi. 44).

From about the fourth century onwards, however, when the church became established and the numbers of clergy and members grew, the procedure for enrolling sinners as penitents and then readmitting them to communion once they had repented was formalised.

Public Repentance

Let us imagine for a moment that we are one of those who at that time were guilty of a grave sin and wished to be absolved.

We go to the bishop of the town in which or near which we live, or to the priest appointed by him to hear confessions, and we tell him what we have done. We do not necessarily confess all our minor sins, only the major offence which is weighing heavily on our conscience.

The cleric lays on us an obligation to undertake certain penitential exercises for a period. If we lived in the east – somewhere like Antioch or Alexandria – the exercise would probably consist of standing near the church door and asking the faithful to pray for us as they assembled for the Sunday eucharist (the length of time we would have to do this would vary with the gravity of our sin: it might be several years). But if we lived in the west – somewhere like Rome or Carthage – the punishment would be shorter and more severe – fasting on certain days, saying extra prayers, wearing penitential garb (hair-shirts and other uncomfortable attire!) and perhaps even living in a monastery for a time. Augustine as bishop gave his penitents unpleasant jobs to do, like burying the dead!

During this period we are allowed to attend the Sunday eucharist, but we are not allowed to join in it in any way. We hear the congregation praying for us in the litanies, but we are not permitted to say the responses with them ('Lord, hear our prayer', or 'Amen'). These liturgical arrangements reinforce the lesson that our sin has excluded us from the Christian community, although they still care for us and pray for our forgiveness.

Being a penitent would seem to us rather like

becoming a catechumen all over again – those weeks before we were baptised, confirmed and received communion for the first time. Lent owes its existence in the Christian year because it was customary during this season for catechumens to be prepared for their initiation at the Easter vigil and for penitents to be prepared for their reconciliation.

Then, before Easter, we approach the priest and ask him if we can be reconciled. He questions us to assure himself that we are truly sorry for our sin and that we have performed the exercise laid on us to the best of our ability. Satisfied about this, he makes arrangements for us to come to church on the day which later came to be called Maundy Thursday for the elaborate ceremonies of reconciliation.

On the appointed day, we stand outside the church door while the congregation arrives. Friends wave to us and show by their smiles that they're glad we're to be received back into the fellowship.

The service starts with the singing of some of the penitential psalms (6, 32, 38, 51, 102, 130 and 143). These are sung with loud shouts of joy: the atmosphere is more like a modern charismatic praise rally than evensong in an Anglican cathedral.

Then the deacon comes out and leads us with the other penitents into the church to present us to the bishop. There we prostrate ourselves on the floor (some bishops prostrated themselves with the penitents as an act of humility to show that they realised they were in constant need of forgiveness, too).

The deacon calls for silence and makes a formal supplication to the bishop on our behalf. The following example comes from an ancient ordinal or bishop's service book which was probably compiled in the thirteenth century. Now in the Vatican library (it is catalogued as 'Vatican 4744'), liturgical scholars believe the texts it contains were in use between the years AD 700 and 900. We note how it weaves together the two themes – baptism ('those to be newly born') and the reconciliation of penitents like us ('those who have returned'):

> The accepted time, O venerable pontiff, is at hand, the day of divine propitiation and human salvation, in which death has received destruction and eternal life a beginning, when in the vineyard of the Lord of Hosts a planting of new shoots is to be made in such a way that the care of the old may be effected by cleansing. We grow by those to be newly born, we increase by those who have returned . . .

When the deacon has finished, the bishop motions us to kneel upright while he lays his hands on the head of each penitent, saying:

> May the almighty and merciful God absolve you from every bond of sin and may you have life everlasting and live through our Lord Jesus Christ. Amen.

In great thankfulness we stand, to be embraced in exchanging the peace with the clergy and with our friends; then we prepare to receive communion at Easter.

Private Repentance

Although such services remained in the books, they gradually fell into disuse except on those rare occasions already mentioned.

One disadvantage was the publicity that attended them. Another was that the church only permitted repentance, like baptism, once in a lifetime. The consequence was that individual sinners postponed repenting, and bishops and priests refused to absolve young people in case they committed another grave sin later in life. Deathbed absolutions were common.

But Jesus Christ had told his disciples that forgiveness was to be offered to those who repented not seven times but seventy-times-seven (meaning an unlimited number), and the church was eventually led by the Holy Spirit to administer absolution more freely among her members.

The change began in the Celtic church in the British Isles at the end of the sixth and the beginning of the seventh century, and from there it spread to the Continent. When Theodore of Tarsus became Archbishop of Canterbury in AD 668, he noticed that absolution was administered differently in this country from what he had been used to in the east. The main differences were that the act of reconciliation was made privately, and that the sinner was absolved not once but as often as he truly repented. So instead of the liturgy of repentance being an act of the whole congregation, it became a simple encounter between the priest and the penitent. It was called 'private penance' to distinguish it from the older 'public penance'. Another name for it was 'auricular confession' – confession made in the priest's 'ear'.

It played an important role in the life of Christians throughout the Middle Ages. Because it was so private it came to be used, not just for the confession of grave sins, but also for the confession of minor faults. This was for two reasons.

First, since the liturgy of repentance now focused on the absolution pronounced by the priest, this came to be regarded as an important – even vital – means of receiving God's grace of forgiveness. Medieval theologians taught that absolution was one of the seven sacraments instituted by Jesus Christ and that every Christian ought to receive that sacrament. By the beginning of the thirteenth century the Fourth Lateran Council (1215) summed up what had become the normal practice in many parts of the west when it decreed: 'Let every one of the faithful . . . confess in secret to his own priest all his sins at least once a year . . .'

Secondly, going to confession came to be associated with spiritual direction, so that the priest was called on not only to assign suitable punishments but also to give advice on a great variety of ethical and ascetical matters. The confessional became the place where the laymen and laywomen bared their souls and relied on the counsel of the priest who now became their 'father confessor'.

A whole theology of salvation based on the practice of private repentance was taught. Mortal sins must be confessed to a priest and absolved, otherwise there was a danger that when the penitent died his soul would have to spend a long period in purgatory being cleansed. Out of the church's 'treasury of merit' the punishment due to the penitent for his sin could be paid off, though he may still have to spend some time in purgatory unless he truly repented and thereafter lived a holy life. Venial sins ought to be confessed, too, though they were not as damaging as mortal sins. The absolution uttered by the priest conveyed spiritual authority to remit the effect of sin in the name of Jesus Christ.

We catch a glimpse of the medieval parish priest hearing confessions in a manual for clergy produced by John Mirk, a member of a religious community at Lilleshall in Shropshire. The earliest manuscript is dated 1450, but it is thought that Mirk lived in the fourteenth century. A feature of his *Instructions for Parish Priests* is that it is written in rhythmic verse. More than half the book is concerned with hearing confessions. The author warned his reader that a 'shrift father' ('shrift' = 'one who shrives [absolves]') should know a good deal more than he has written in the book and that he should pray to God for guidance.

When a man comes to confession the priest must make sure that he comes from his own parish. Priests in religious communities were allowed to hear anyone's confession, but normally penitents were expected to go to their own parish priest. They could go elsewhere if the priest was known to be immoral or if the sins they wished to confess involved the priest personally or his near relatives. (John Mirk suggested that a penitent should go to someone else if his sins were connected with the parish priest's mother, sister, daughter or concubine – a sidelight on the lives of at least a few medieval priests!)

When the penitent is a woman, the priest must take care not to look at her. He should pull his hood over his eyes and sit as 'still as stone'; he should not cough, spit, or fidget with his 'shanks' in case she thinks he is shocked by what he hears. If she hesitates, he should encourage her by saying:

> Do not hold it back for shame,
> For, perhaps, I've done the same –
> And most probably much more
> If thou couldst know all my sore.

He must see if the penitent knows the Paternoster, the Ave Maria and the creed. If there is time, he should help him make a self-examination y questioning him on the ten commandments and the deadly sins, and he should explain to the penitent that the circumstances of his sins must be confessed – *quis? quod? ubi? per quos? quociens? quomodo? quando?* (who? what? where? with whom? how often? in what way? when?).

A priest is never to impose heavy punishments. There is always a danger that the penitent will fail to complete them and so be in a worse condition than if he had not gone to confession. It is better to send a man to purgatory by imposing a light sentence than to send him to hell by giving a severe one that he is unable to fulfil. A woman's punishment should be of such a kind that her husband will not know of it.

The antidote to mortal sins are the cardinal virtues. For example, a proud man would be given a punishment that teaches him to be humble:

> Oft to kneel, and earth to kiss,
> Knowing well that dust he is,
> And dead man's bones oft to see
> And think that he shall such be.

Reform

These teachings and practices were attacked by the Reformers in the sixteenth century. They said the distinction between mortal and venial sin was unscriptural. John Calvin wrote:

> We, as the scripture teaches us, declare that the wages of sin is death, and that the soul that has sinned is worthy of death; moreover, that the sins of the faithful are venial: not that they do not merit death, but inasmuch as in the mercy of God there is no condemnation to them which are in Christ Jesus: inasmuch as their sins are not imputed to them, but are blotted out by grace.
>
> (*Insitutes*, III, 4, 28)

Furthermore, the whole practice was riddled with abuses. Penances imposed on the wealthy and powerful were undertaken by servants or serfs for a payment. The giving of the absolution was seen not so much as reconciliation with God and the church as a power of the keys exercised by the priest in virtue of his ordination and office. It was sale of indulgences in Germany which prompted Martin Luther to protest in 1517 – the date which marks the beginning of the Reformation.

The churches which sprang from the Reformation did not completely abolish auricular confession as such. Martin Luther commended it in his Great Catechism (1529), not as obligatory but as a means of pastoral care: 'When the heart is sorrowing for its sins and longs for consolation, it finds here a sure refuge, where it hears the Word of God, and learns that God, through the ministry of man, looses and absolves it from its sins.'

The Church of England similarly commended the practice for those whose consciences troubled them, and she retained a medieval absolution formula in the Prayer Book:

> Our Lord Jesus Christ, who hath left power to his church to absolve all sinners who truly repent and believe in him, of his great mercy forgive thee thine offences: and by his authority committed to me, I absolve thee from all thy sins, in the name of the Father, and of the Son, and of the Holy Ghost. Amen.
>
> (*The Visitation of the Sick*)

Anglican Evangelicals have long campaigned for a revision of the absolution formula, pointing out that the indicative, 'I absolve thee', has no scriptural authority. It is this campaign which has held up the Church of England's revision of the rite for reconciliation.

The priests of the eastern churches heard confessions, but their teaching and practice has been more like that of the Anglican church. The priest and the penitent stand in the church at a desk on which is placed a cross or an icon of the Saviour or the book of the gospels; the priest stands slightly to one side. This arrangement emphasises that in confession the priest is not a judge but only a witness and God's minister.

When the confession has been made, the priest places his stole on the penitent's head and then, laying his hand on the stole, says the prayer of absolution. It is not indicative ('I forgive . . .') but deprecative ('May God forgive . . .').

> Whatever you have said to my humble person, and whatever you have failed to say, whether through ignorance or forgetfulness, whatever it may be, may God forgive you in this world and in the next . . . Have no further anxiety; go in peace.

The rule about going to confession has remained in the Roman Catholic church, but the juridical nature of the discipline is gradually disappearing. This process was accelerated after the publication of the papal encyclical, *Humanae vitae*, in 1967 banning the use of artificial means of contraception. Legally speaking, Roman Catholic couples who used contraceptives were excommunicated unless they made their confessions and gave up the practice. Most did not. They either ceased to go to confession (and to Mass in many cases) or they made their confessions to priests who were known to be sympathetic and who would absolve them even though they used contraceptives in planning their families.

The revised Roman rites which were published in 1973 have a strongly pastoral character, and going to confession in that church is now very similar to elsewhere. Today confessions are heard by priests in informal ways, usually sitting with the penitent and praying together afterwards. Absolution is often given with the laying on of hands.

The Roman Catholic church in recent years has experimented with 'services of penitence' in which Bible readings, an address, a penitential litany and other prayers have been used in Lent and as preparation for Easter – individuals making their confessions to the priest privately afterwards if they wished.

These changes have made the practice more what its title indicates it should be – a ministry of reconciliation for those who need the prayers of the church in finding peace with God and with their Christian brothers and sisters, especially after crises of doubt and disobedience in their lives.

It is no longer confined to Catholic and Orthodox traditions. Members of the Reformed churches have discovered the grace of God in confessing sins to a minister. Richard Foster describes how he made his first confession. For about ten minutes on each of three days he noted down his sins of childhood, youth and early adult life. Then he went to a 'dear brother in Christ' and confessed the sins he had written down. The other took the piece of paper, tore it into tiny shreds, and put it in the wastepaper basket. 'That powerful nonverbal expression of forgiveness was followed by a simple absolution. My sins I knew were as far away as the east is from the west' (*Celebration of Discipline*, 1980, p. 131).

So this ministry is available for all who are troubled by the kind of doubts listed at the end of the last chapter. It is not an easy discipline to undertake, but the blessings which flow from it are far-reaching. When we've made our confession to another, we experience the joy and freedom of those who've heard the Lord's word of forgiveness.

The use of set prayers for such occasions releases us from the anxiety of wondering what we ought to say. Since many readers may not be familiar with them, I will conclude this chapter by printing the form for the ministry of reconciliation which has been authorised by the Anglican Church in Canada in the Book of Alternative Services (1985). Note how scripture passages are incorporated into it (and there is provision for more) and how the priest's formula has been revised to remove the 'I absolve thee' phrase from it (surely an admirable example for the Church of England to satisfy Evangelical objections?).

THE RECONCILIATION OF A PENITENT

Priest   Bless the Lord who forgives all our sins.

Penitent His mercy endures for ever.

The priest invites the penitent to trust God, in these or similar words,

        May God, who enlightens every heart, help you to confess your sins and to trust in his mercy.

Penitent Most merciful God, have mercy upon me,
        in your compassion forgive my sins,
           both known and unknown,
        things done and left undone,
           (especially . . .)
        O God, uphold me by your Spirit
        that I may live and serve you in newness
           of life,
        to the honour and glory of your name;
           through Jesus Christ, our Lord. Amen.

The priest may, with the consent of the penitent, offer words of comfort and counsel, and then says,

> Our Lord Jesus Christ, who offered himself as the perfect sacrifice to the Father, and who conferred power on his Church to forgive sins, absolve you through my ministry by the grace of the Holy Spirit, and restore you in the perfect peace of the Church. Amen.

A deacon or lay person says, instead of the absolution, this declaration of forgiveness,

> Our Lord Jesus Christ, who offered himself as the perfect sacrifice to the Father, forgives our sins and grants us the grace and comfort of the Holy Spirit. Amen.

The priest then dismisses the penitent,

> Blessed are they whose trangressions are forgiven;

Penitent And whose sin is put away.

Priest The Lord has put away all your sins.

Penitent Thanks be to God

Then the priest concludes,

> Go in peace, and pray for me a sinner.

For Discussion

(1) Is the modern church slack in not disciplining more strictly those who fall into grave sin?

(2) Would you find it easier to make your confession to a trusted lay Christian friend than to an ordained minister?

2 Corinthians 5.15–6.2

verses 16–21 *We once regarded Christ in this way*:
that is, the world's way. *New
creation*: forgiveness leads to the
fulfilment of God's purposes in
creating the world. *Ministers of
reconciliation*: we who receive
God's reconciliation have the privi-
lege of being his messengers of it to
others. *Made him who had no sin
to be sin for us*: Christ took the
results of our sin so that we could
receive his righteousness.

1–2 *To receive God's grace in vain*: e.g.,
by living for oneself. *He says*:
quotation from Isaiah 49.8. Those
who were faithful to God in the OT
received the promises that were
later fulfilled in Christ and therefore
entered into salvation (see John
8.56 and Hebrews 11.13).

7

Reconciliation

During a visit to Holland some years ago, I visited an elderly Dutch Christian in his home in the suburbs of The Hague. While he was in the kitchen making a cup of coffee, I noticed a number of holes in the wooden beams of the ceiling of the living room where I was sitting. When he returned, I pointed to them and asked if they were war damage.

He poured out the coffee and sat down before he answered my question.

During the Second World War, he told me, the Nazis had rounded up young Dutchmen for forced labour camps in Germany. His son had not been old enough for this in the early years of the German occupation, but during this time the father and son constructed a hiding-place between that ceiling and the floor of the bedroom above. Then, as the boy's birthday drew near, the parents let it be known that their son had gone to live with relatives in Luxembourg. In fact, the boy remained with them. He stayed indoors during daylight hours, venturing out only after dark.

One evening the boy was spotted in the garden by a neighbour, who reported what he had seen to the Germans. Fortunately the parents were warned that their house was about to be searched and they put the boy in the hiding-place above the ceiling.

Questioned by two German officers, the parents denied any knowledge of a boy in the garden, sticking to their story that their son had gone away. The Germans made a brief search of the house. Just before they left, however, one of them pointed an automatic rifle at the ceiling and fired a few short bursts. Nothing happened, and the Germans departed. The boy had not been hit. It was only a few months later that Holland was liberated by the Allies.

'That,' concluded the Dutchman, 'was how the bullet-holes appeared in our ceiling.'

'What happened to your neighbour?' I asked.

He pointed out of the window. Through the trees and shrubs dividing my host's garden from the grounds of the house next door I could see an old man pushing an electric lawnmower.

'Is that the same man?'

He nodded.

'Didn't you denounce him as a collaborator after the war?'

He shrugged his shoulders. 'There had been enough suffering by the time we were liberated. . . And, besides, Christians must forgive. . .'

I looked out of the window again. The neighbour was still pushing his lawnmower. Thirty or more years ago he had nearly brought about the deportation or death of my host's son; and yet these two men were still living next door to one another, not on intimate terms but with that reserve and tolerance which characterises people who live in the more expensive suburbs of north Europe.

The Dutchman had forgiven his neighbour's betrayal. And he had maintained that forgiving attitude for the long years afterwards, even though the memory of it remained, with the signs in the ceiling of his house. He had, I thought, experienced more than one kind of liberation. Besides being freed from the Nazis, he had entered into the liberation of those who share with others the forgiveness of God.

God's gift of forgiveness is not meant to stop with us. He expects us to pass it on. Just as he shows mercy and grants forgiveness to us, we are to become a people who show mercy and grant forgiveness to others.

Throughout this book I've stressed that the essential thing about forgiveness is that it is God's free gift to us. I've also stressed that forgiveness is much more than wiping our slate clean: it's essentially a gift from God of restored relationships with him: 'We are justified freely by his grace through the redemption that came by Jesus Christ' (Romans 3.24).

The gift of God – like all his gifts – is a gift to be shared. For if ever we are tempted to think of God's gifts as graces for ourselves alone, then we are no longer channels of his Spirit. If we're not overflowing with all that God sends us, we are not receiving all he sends, either. Christ taught this in one of the great moments of his ministry in the fourth gospel:

On the last and greatest day of the feast, Jesus stood and said in a loud voice, 'If anyone is thirsty, let him come to me and drink. Whoever believes in me, as the scripture has said, streams of living water will flow from within him.' By this he meant the Spirit, whom those who believed in him were later to receive.

(John 7.37–39)

This particular passage is usually related to the outpouring of the gifts of the Spirit on the church following the feast of Pentecost. But it applies to the gift of forgiveness as well. To receive the gift of forgiveness is like the receiving of any other spiritual gift. It is for the common good.

Jesus constantly stressed this in his teaching – most forcibly in the parable of the unmerciful servant. This parable is part of a series of sayings about forgiveness, and it was a 'kingdom of heaven' parable – that is to say, a story to demonstrate how the rule of Christ is to be reflected in our lives.

A king found that a certain servant owed him millions of pounds (the vast sum representing the impossible 'debt' that we owe God). The servant begged him, 'Be patient with me, and I will pay back everything' (Matthew 18.26). Of course, the servant had no hope of doing that: the sum was too big (just as it is impossible for us to pay back to God the immense 'debt' we owe him because of our sins). The king realised this, but nevertheless he cancelled the debt. But when the king heard later that the same servant had committed to prison a fellow-servant who owed him a few pounds, the king had him thrown into prison, too. Then came the punch-line in the parable:

'This is how my heavenly Father will treat each of you unless you forgive your brother from your heart' (Matthew 18.35).

Jesus also linked God's forgiveness of us with our willingness to forgive others in his prayer: 'Forgive us our sins, as we also forgive everyone who sins against us' (Luke 11.4). Which means that if we're not forgiving, we can't pray as Jesus taught us to pray.

Love v. Hatred

Unwillingness to forgive – where pride dominates rather than love – is a seedbed for all kinds of troubles, spiritual as well as psychological (which, in their turn, frequently manifest themselves in physical disorders). Not being willing to forgive another ultimately means that we hate another. To say we are indifferent towards that person is a delusion. There is no neutrality in a relationship where feelings have been hurt.

On a spiritual level such hatred can be a door for Satan to enter and create havoc in our lives. Often those who seek deliverance from the power of evil have to be helped to forgive a past hurt they received from someone – such as a father who abused them, or a mother who deserted them.

Hatred leads to a descent into a personal hell of inordinate self-love (often linked with self-pity) which manifests itself by an attachment to a particular sin, or a trek through the occult. It is frightening to think of how many of the world's tyrants have been responsible for untold suffering because they gave themselves up to hatred and put behind them any notion of forgiveness.

Psychologically hatred results in all kinds of twisted attitudes and behaviour, which show themselves in various physical and mental disorders. One of the reasons why the ministry of healing is spreading in the church today is because those who are sick are learning how necessary it is to be forgiven and to forgive.

Yet an unwillingness to forgive crops up in the most unexpected places. Early in my experience of an ecumenical ministry I was asked to visit a group of about thirty or so members of a congregation who had broken away from their parent church.

I met them one evening to listen to their story. There had been a sharp division of opinion in the congregation to which they belonged over a matter of pastoral strategy, and since they were without a minister at the time, there was no one to help them through the difficulty. Feelings ran high, and in the end one group – the people I met – broke away and began gathering for worship in one another's homes.

They had been doing this for several months when consciences started to prick and they wondered if they should be doing something to try and heal the division. From their point of view, they believed the stand they had taken in the dispute had been justified; but they were concerned at the signs of bitterness which had grown up between them and the remainder of the congregation. Lifelong friendships had been broken; members of a family were not on speaking terms.

It was at this point that they invited me to visit them. I listened to their story for an hour or more. Then I suggested we spent a few minutes in silence while we sought the Lord's guiding.

During those minutes a thought of what I should say to them came into my mind. At first it made me shrink, for I knew I wouldn't be popular if I suggested it. But the more I tried to put it behind me, the more it impressed itself on me, so I came to the reluctant conclusion that maybe it was what the Lord wanted me to say after all!

When I opened my eyes they were all looking at me – like devotees waiting for an oracle. I hesitated; then I said what I'd been thinking:

'I believe the Lord is saying to you that you're to go back to your church and tell them that you're sorry before God for having been involved in this division. I know you feel the fault was theirs rather than yours; but I don't think you can claim you were entirely free from blame for what has happened. After all, you did walk out on them without waiting to see if you couldn't all be reconciled in some way.

'When you've done this, I suggest you offer to take part with them in a service of reconciliation. I'll help you to organise it, if it would help. When that's over, you should then take time to discuss the future with them. It might be right for you to continue as two separate congregations, for the differences between you are considerable, and God may be calling you to a separate ministry. Or it might be right for you to join up again.'

There was a long pause after I'd finished. I sensed coolness and hostility! But then one voice spoke up: 'He's right, you know! He's right!'

I left them shortly after that. Months later I learned that they hadn't followed up my suggestion. They were continuing as a separate group. I wondered that such a group of seemingly nice Christian people could be so unforgiving. I wasn't surprised when I learned a few years later that their numbers had dwindled until in the end they stopped meeting altogether.

On the other hand, where there is forgiveness between Christians, the result is a powerful witness to the cross of Jesus Christ and the loving mercy of God.

There was an ecumenical rally in the town hall of a northern city during the Week of Prayer for Christian Unity. The clergy were seated in a semicircle round the platform. Just before the intercessions, a young Pentecostal pastor came to the microphone and said that before we prayed he wished to make an announcement. Turning to the Roman Catholic priest, he asked for his forgiveness for all the evil thoughts and fears he (the pastor) had had of the priest's church. He felt that unless he made such a confession, he could never enter into a unity of the Spirit with Roman Catholics.

The Roman Catholic priest stood up and walked to the microphone. He also asked the Pentecostal pastor to forgive him for all the evil thoughts and fears which he (the priest) had had about the Pente-costal church and Protestant churches as well.

The two men shook hands, and people in the audience took that as a cue to give one another the peace. It was an emotional moment, during which I sensed many barriers falling down between the different congregations in that city.

There needs to be much more of that kind of thing before the movement for Christian unity can become a movement for the kingdom of God in our cities, towns and villages. If our Roman Catholic friends can teach us to adapt their services of penitence to such occasions, they will be helping us to receive great blessings from the Lord.

Restoration

I did not hear any more of the Dutchman's story, except that his wife had died some years previously and that his son was now married and living in another part of Holland. But those bullet-holes remained in the ceiling – a sign that although we forgive, we may not be able to forget.

When we've wronged someone, or when someone has wronged us, and that wrong has caused deep hurts, it is impossible to turn back the clock and have it the way it was. Such hurts cannot be obliter-ated. To pretend that it never happened is unre-alistic. The consequences of that wrong will always be between us, no matter how penitent we are or how forgiving the other is.

But we can be reconciled together. That is why it is important to grasp the difference between reconciliation and restoration. We repent and we confess – and then go on to build the relationship anew. It is beyond our human capacities, even when aided by God's grace, to restore the relationship to exactly what it was before, yet a new relationship can be born out of the old when there has been forgiveness.

The difference between reconciliation and restoration is like the difference between singing in unison and singing in harmony. Two people who have never offended one another are like two choirboys singing in unison: their voices blend perfectly and they sound as if they were one. But once there has been an offence between them, then that unity has been broken. They can be reconciled through confession and forgiveness, but they can never return to that unity which they had before. A different kind of unity has to be built up between them – like two choirboys singing in harmony.

This is an important distinction in all kinds of personal reconciliations – not least in working through marriage difficulties. An act of infidelity, for example, by one or both partners is never likely to be forgotten; but the marriage can be rescued – and a new and frequently richer unity with one another entered into – if there is reconciliation. This will not restore old relationships, but it will provide a bridge over which love can flow. And love is the necessary ingredient to create reconciliation.

God's forgiveness, however, goes further. He *does* restore as well as reconcile. He not only forgives our sins; he blots them out. They are no longer a factor in our relationships with him; they died in the death of Jesus Christ. That is why Paul, seeing our sins placarded against us in terms of having broken God's commandments, also saw them extinguished by the cross: 'God forgave our sins, having cancelled the written code, with its regulations, that was against us and that stood opposed to us; he took it away, nailing it to the cross' (Colossians 2.14).

To be justified in God's sight means being restored as well as reconciled. Justification, in the theological sense, calls for the recreation of a situation as it was before the break in relationships between God and ourselves happened. The memory of what it was that caused the break has to be wiped out for justification to be complete. And this is what God does in his mercy. He acts towards us as if we hadn't sinned. 'I will forgive their wickedness and will remember their sins no more' (Jeremiah 31.34). It is not only possible to be reconciled with God, it is possible to have the old relationship, as seen in the garden of Eden, fully restored.

A Sign of Forgiveness

When he reconciles us to himself in Christ, God calls us to be ministers of reconciliation in his world. No longer sinners under the old creation, we are to be a people of reconciliation in his new creation:

> Therefore, if anyone is in Christ, he is a new creation; the old has gone, the new has come! All this is from God, who reconciled us to himself through Christ and gave us the ministry of reconciliation: that God was reconciling the world to himself in Christ, not counting men's sins against them. And he has committed to us the message of reconciliation. We are therefore Christ's ambassadors, as though God were making his appeal through us. We implore you on Christ's behalf: be reconciled to God.
>
> (2 Corinthians 5.17–20)

It is the world that God was reconciling to himself in Christ, and that message of reconciliation is committed to the church, those who are experiencing

113

that reconciliation among themselves as well as in their individual relationship with God. If the church is to be a credible ambassador for Christ, then we who are members of the church have to be a sign of that forgiveness, that reconciliation, for the world to see. We need to be a community of love which becomes a light set on a stand.

Society is riddled with divisions and hatreds which cry out for God's gifts of forgiveness and healing. But society rarely listens to what the church has to say; it is what the church is and what we do that proclaims the message of the Gospel most effectively. The most powerful sermons are spoken by what we experience rather than what we hear. These are the signs and wonders which the world notices.

In a countless number of incidents the message depends on the willingness of ordinary church members to take risks as Christ's ambassadors in the places where they live and work and spend their time. In my ministry I learn of many such examples. I will mention two.

The first was in the early 1980s, when the riots in Toxteth sparked off similar disturbances in Moss Side and Hulme in Manchester, and there was a growing sense of suspicion and hostility towards the police among certain sections of the black community.

Through various links which had been formed with the Greater Manchester County Ecumenical Council (the body which employs me as its secretary) it was possible to arrange a meeting between representatives of the black churches and senior officers from the Greater Manchester Police. About sixty pastors and leaders from the black churches came together with seven senior police officers and a similar number of GMCEC members. After a meal together, we divided into small groups with one policeman to every seven or eight black Christians, and one member of the GMCEC as a chairperson.

In my group two of the black pastors described incidents in which they claimed they were harassed by the police. One man owned a lorry which he drove to market early each morning to collect fruit and vegetables to distribute to a number of shops. One day a police car had stopped him on suspicion his brakes were not working. But when the police tested them, they were found to be in order. They had taken a long time over this and he had got agitated, saying he would be late for market. At this they laughed and proceeded to make other checks on the lorry, delaying him for half an hour. Before they let him go, they told him they were going to stop him every morning for the rest of the week.

The other pastor, a mother of six children, claimed that her twenty-year-old son had been taken to a police station to be searched for drugs. In the following weeks he had been harassed by the same constables who searched him whenever they saw him. She had visited the station and complained, but nothing had been done.

When they had finished, the chief superintendent sitting beside me was silent for a while. Then he looked round the group and told them he was sorry for the behaviour of the officers he'd heard about. He said he wanted to apologise on behalf of the force to those who felt they had been unjustly treated. He told them that if anything like that happened again, they were to ring his number in the county police headquarters and he would deal with the matter directly.

The other groups had similar experiences. Out of that meeting arrangements were made for one or two of the black pastors to participate in the training of young constables. Later the Home Office authorised a black pastor to visit any police station.

Although it was only a minor incident in a highly complex situation, nevertheless the pastors reported to us months later that the relationships between their congregations and the police were remarkably improved. And I've no doubt it was the apology which they received at the meeting which had done much to help that.

The second example was when I attended a renewal meeting two or three years ago in Newry, the town on the border between Northern Ireland and the Irish Republic which has suffered many bombings, killings and woundings in the troubles of the last twenty years. The meeting was held in a large church hall with about two hundred people present. I spoke about the relationship between renewal and repentance, and then I invited the audience to join in prayer.

Just as silence settled in the room, a man sitting near the front on my right stood up and began to speak. I cannot remember his exact words, but they were something like this:

'Friends, before we pray, I believe I need to share something with you. I want you to know that until two years ago I was an officer in the Ulster Volunteer Force [an illegal Protestant paramilitary organisation]. I used to think it was my duty to shoot Roman Catholics, and I carried a gun so that I could do that.'

A gasp went round the hall. One or two of those sitting near him instinctively edged away.

'But then Jesus Christ spoke to me,' he continued, 'and I realised how grievously I was sinning. I resigned from the UVF, threw my gun into a river, and now I am part of a prayer group with Roman

Catholics. We meet every week and they are my dearest brothers and sisters in Christ.'

He sat down, and there was a spontaneous burst of clapping and cries of 'Praise the Lord!' I was deeply moved. Such a public confession is so unlikely in Northern Ireland.

But that was not all. As the applause died down, another man stood up on the other side of the room. I lifted a hand to silence the audience and nodded to him.

'I thank my brother for what he has shared with us,' he said. 'And I want to share something, too. I come from Monaghan [a town with strong republican sympathies over the border] and I used to be in the IRA. I, too, heard Christ speak to me, and I resigned from the army. I want to ask my brother over there for his forgiveness for all the hatred I used to have for Protestants like him in the north.'

At this, he walked out to the front with his arms outstretched, and the former UVF officer also came forward. The two men embraced and wept on one another's shoulders like long lost brothers. For me and for everyone present it was a powerful prophetic sign that forgiveness in the love of God can overcome the deepest and bitterest of human hatreds. When people say that only the Lord can solve the problems of Northern Ireland, I want to tell them I've seen him doing just that!

The Spirit's Power

Reconciliations such as these can only happen through the power of the Holy Spirit. The church can only be a sign of forgiveness through the continual indwelling of the Spirit, to become a herald of the new creation, God's kingdom, in midst of the old.

So for me a book like this, which focuses just on God's gift of forgiveness, is in some ways unsatisfactory. That isn't because I regard such a gift as unimportant! Certainly not! It's because I feel I've only mentioned one side of Christian discipleship.

That gift of God to us through Christ, tremendous as it is, is just a preliminary. It clears the way for the permanent indwelling of the Holy Spirit, both in our personal lives and in the corporate life of the church. For being a follower of Jesus Christ is not just about being forgiven. It's about living and worshipping and loving and serving in the victory which was won in his death and resurrection and which is shared with us through the power of Pentecost.

That's what equips the church to be a sign of God's forgiveness in the world.

Jesus taught that once a man is delivered of an evil spirit, he is in danger of being troubled by seven worse spirits unless he is filled with the Holy Spirit (Matthew 12.43–45). The same is true for us when we have repented. If we only seek the forgiveness of God, we will be cleansed of our former sins; but there will be a spiritual vacuum in our lives until we are being filled with the Holy Spirit.

That is why I would like to go on to say more about yielding ourselves each day to the Holy Spirit. But I set myself the task of writing about the forgiveness of sins, and it must be left to other books to discuss living in the Spirit and other aspects of Christian discipleship. My purpose has been to expound what Jesus meant when he said:

I tell you the truth, everyone who sins is a slave to sin. Now a slave has no permanent place in the family, but a son belongs to it for ever. So if the Son sets you free, you will be free indeed.

(John 8.34–36)

118

So I will end with one more story which tells how an act of forgiveness prepared for a manifestation of the Spirit's power, and in one of the most Anglican ways imaginable – through a confirmation service! It is also a Second World War story, and it is about Leonard Wilson, later to become Bishop of Birmingham.

Wilson was captured by the Japanese in Singapore and held a prisoner in the notorious Changi gaol. There he suffered as so many Allied prisoners did at the hands of the Japanese. On one occasion, in October 1943, he was taken for torture. Recalling the floggings he had endured years before at his public school – one established especially for the sons of the clergy – he said to himself as it began, 'Well, thank heavens I went to St John's, Leatherhead!'

'When I muttered "Forgive them",' Wilson went on, 'I wondered how far I was being dramatic and if I really meant it, because I looked at their faces as they stood round and took it in turn to flog, and their faces were hard and cruel and some of them were evidently enjoying their cruelty.

'But by the grace of God I saw those men not as they were, but as they had been. Once they were little children playing with their brothers and sisters and happy in their parents' love, in those far-off days before they had been conditioned by their false nationalist ideals, and it is hard to hate little children. But even that was not enough. There came to my mind as I lay on the table the words of that communion hymn:

> Look, Father, look on His anointed face,
> And only look on us as found in Him.

'And so I saw them, not as they had been, but as they were capable of becoming, redeemed by the

119

power of Christ, and I knew that it was only common sense to say "forgive".'

Years later, as a bishop, Wilson laid his hands on the head of one of his Japanese captors who was kneeling before him at a confirmation service and prayed that he might receive the gift of the Holy Spirit.

For Discussion

(1) What experience have you had of forgiveness and reconciliation in local churches?

(2) Do you think there is any difference between the forgiveness offered by a Christian and that offered by one who is not a believer?

Bible Reading

2 Samuel 18.19–33

verses 10–23   Joab, one of the commanders of King David's army, despatched to put down the rebellion of David's son, Absalom, heard that Absalom had been killed (18.9). He despatched a Cushite messenger to take the news to David, but he allowed Ahimaaz to go as well, though he felt the latter was not a suitable person to convey bad news to the king.

14–33   David saw the two messengers coming and assumed they brought good news. Ahimaaz could not bring himself to tell him of Absalom's death, so it was left to the second messenger to do that. The story is one where death prevented any repentance and reconciliation between David and his son. *O my son Absalom!* – one of the most famous passages in the Bible of a father mourning for a disobedient son.

TWISTED STRANDS

Vicki thought her happiness was complete; she lived with her parents and young brother, Matt, on the family flower farm — beautifully situated on an island off the south-west coast of England — and was engaged to Steve, who lived nearby. But when her beautiful sister, Catriona, came back home from London, Vicki's life was thrown into turmoil — she overheard Steve telling Catriona that he still loved her. How could things ever be the same again?

Books by Patricia Freer
in the Linford Romance Library:

WHEN TOMORROW COMES
CHARMING DECEPTION
A THING OF BEAUTY

PATRICIA FREER

TWISTED
STRANDS

Complete and Unabridged

LINFORD
Leicester

First published in Great Britain

First Linford Edition
published 2001

The moral right of the author
has been asserted

British Library CIP Data

Freer, Patricia
　　Twisted strands.—Large print ed.—
　　Linford romance library
　　1. Love stories
　　2. Large type books
　　I. Title
　　823.9′14 [F]

　　ISBN 0–7089–5932–6

Published by
F. A. Thorpe (Publishing)
Anstey, Leicestershire

Set by Words & Graphics Ltd.
Anstey, Leicestershire
Printed and bound in Great Britain by
T. J. International Ltd., Padstow, Cornwall

This book is printed on acid-free paper

1

Vicki Jamieson stood up, stretching her aching back, and gazed across to the path by the hedge. There was a man walking across it, a stranger to her as far as she could tell from that distance. Strictly speaking, he was trespassing but most of the islanders used that path as a right of way.

He stood still and raised a pair of binoculars. Looking for ships, Vicki supposed, without much interest. She returned her gaze to her brother, Matt, and missed the swing of the binoculars as they were shifted and trained on her.

From the pugnacious set of Matt's chin, she realised she'd have to use all her diplomatic skills to wheedle a full day's work out of him. Secretly she sympathised. It was Sunday — he'd worked hard all day yesterday, and what Father paid was no incentive. She put on her big-sister-needs-you voice.

'Matt, get a move on. We must finish this field today. The weather may break tomorrow.'

'It's so hot! Come on, how about a quick swim to cool off?'

'In February! You'd freeze to death. Anyway, it's almost lunchtime. Maybe later this afternoon, if we finish, you can go down to the beach.'

'Do we have to stop for lunch? If we carry on picking now, I could take a picnic. Morley and Pete are going fishing.'

'Come on, only a few more rows, then this field's done. You know if we catch the early markets, we'll get a good price, and the weather's in our favour. And yes, we do have to stop for Sunday lunch. You know Father likes us to eat together on Sundays. It's traditional.'

Matt's fourteen-year-old logic didn't accept that. Just because it was Sunday, he couldn't see the point of sitting down at the same time every week to the same old dinner — roast beef,

Yorkshire pudding, burnt potatoes and mushy vegetables!

'It's not my tradition. My tradition is to have a picnic by the sea on a fine day and eat later in the evening. At my lodgings, the Truscotts always do that. Much more civilised. So does Aunt Cecily. She always refuses to come for Sunday dinner. I expect she's busy on her boat, right now. She won't stop for anything. Why should I?'

Vicki stooped again to pick the tightly-budded daffodils. The last thing she wanted was to break the rhythm of the arduous picking, and go indoors for a huge, midday meal. It was probably the last thing anyone wanted, except Father. Her mother hated cooking, too. She much preferred to be outdoors, painting.

'Aunt Cecily doesn't live with us — she's a law to herself — and she's a lot older than you. When you're her age, I daresay you'll have established your own traditions.'

'Roll on that day,' Matt muttered,

and Vicki came over to put her arm affectionately round his shoulder.

'Don't wish your youth away. It'll be gone soon enough. Bet you anything that when you're older you'll look back on family Sunday lunch as the best time of your life.'

'You're joking!' Her brother's look of disbelief made her laugh.

'Well, not the best maybe. But you might feel a twinge of nostalgia occasionally. Come on — no need to stop picking. Catch me up and we can talk as we go. Time'll pass faster then.'

'Huh! I thought I'd managed to distract you.'

With a resigned look, Matt Jamieson, a gangly betwixt-and-between teenager, bent his long back and began to snip his way down the rows, catching up on his sister, piling up the green stalks. Once moving, he developed a swift, practiced pace, and was soon forging ahead.

Turning his curly, blond head, he grinned wickedly over his shoulder.

4

'Slowcoach. Can't you go any faster?'

'Easily. I can beat you any day.'

Vicki was relieved to have restored his good humour and increased her own pace, glad to make a game out of the back-breaking job.

Piperidge Farm, acres of lush land sprawling over an island off the South West coast of England, had been in the Jamieson family for generations. It was a beauty spot in its own right, and had, for decades, been sending early spring flowers to the mainland. Run mainly by family labour, it had shown good profits in the past when there had been lots of Jamieson children, but now the farm was run by Vicki, her father, and the reluctant young Matthew — when available!

'Beat you,' he called gleefully and Vicki was struck by the speed of his mood changes.

At this moment, he was an excited, young child, yet that could change in a second, especially when he and his father got together! All part of the growing-up process, she supposed.

'Well done! Only just, though. Race you on the next row?'

'You're on. What's the prize? Skip lunch?'

'Matt!' She couldn't help laughing. 'No, but definitely a couple of hours off this afternoon.'

'Done.'

Then he was off, highly motivated. Vicki started to follow, then straightened in dismay at the clang of Father's fifteen-minute warning bell.

The tall, well-built figure would be standing outside the front door of the farmhouse, arms swinging powerfully up and down, calling them in with the old ship's bell he'd salvaged years ago from a wreck. That bell was part of her childhood. She'd never liked it then, and hated it now. It was no good protesting that they all had watches, and were quite capable of regulating their own day.

'Just a whim of mine,' he'd say. 'Part of the old traditions — it doesn't hurt

6

to keep them going.'

The Sunday-dinner bell would ring at five-minute intervals. The last one meant they were to be at the house ready for the meal at half-past twelve — that was if Mother had managed to co-ordinate meat and veg to time! Even if she hadn't, the family had to be assembled at the table on the dot.

Vicki had pleaded dispensation at busy times like now! Absurdly hot for late February, the sun had brought the daffodils into fat, green bud — ideal conditions. Vicki remembered one year in February, picking in a blizzard to save the blooms from damage. But even then, they'd stopped for Sunday lunch!

Father was set in concrete on the issue, and it was becoming a bone of family contention. She'd been aware of Matt's discontent for some time. He was carrying on working, as though the bell had galvanised him into even speedier picking. Hands and clippers skipped deftly along the rows. What a shame to stop him! It would be hard to re-motivate him after dinner.

'Matt — dinner bell,' she called, reluctantly.

'I heard it. I'll just finish this row. See you in there.'

His voice was casual, but she wasn't deceived. Her young brother was trying it on, and she was the first easy hurdle. She sighed. Not today Matt — not with so much to do! A family confrontation was the last thing she needed. It would mean good-bye to a snatched hour riding with Steve later. Her heart lightened at the prospect of galloping across the cliff top on Fleury. She loved the temporary freedom it gave her, freedom from both the responsibilities of the farm and the family.

Matt had been kicking against the restrictions ever since he'd gone away to mainland school and been a weekly boarder with the Truscott family. She'd met the Truscotts and been impressed by the relaxed, happy-go-lucky attitude the parents had with their three children. Matt, having tasted a small measure of freedom during the week, didn't relish week-end restrictions. He used to love coming home for the holidays, but this time he'd been bored from day one! The island wouldn't hold him much longer.

Catriona, their sister, had escaped years ago. If Matt followed, Vicki would be left to fly the flag single-handed. Even marrying Steve wouldn't make much difference — they'd only be a few miles down the road.

'Come in with me,' she said. 'You know Father won't start dinner until we're all there.'

'All! There's only two of us now. He's living in the past, when everyone had about a dozen kids. You know Father's trouble, Vicki? He fancies himself a Victorian patriarch. No other fathers behave like him.'

'You mustn't talk about him that way. It's the first Sunday of your half-term holiday — a special day.'

'Come off it, Vicki. I'm home every Sunday. Worse luck,' he muttered under

9

his breath, feeling thankful that the island was too small to have a secondary school.

At least that meant going to the mainland for weekdays. He wondered if he could persuade Father to let him stay all term. He'd miss Vicki, of course, and Aunt Cecily, and the riding, sailing, swimming, but it'd all be here in the summer. Whereas the winter . . . he pulled a face, and then saw his sister's worried frown.

Standing among the flowers, tall and slender, her shining hair ruffling in the breeze, she put him in mind of a modern-day Scarlett O' Hara in her struggle to survive and work her land. She'd always been a good sister and he knew that he'd be unable to resist the pleading in her velvet-brown eyes.

'OK, you win — this time.'

That satisfied his honour, and told her he wasn't beaten, just postponing the battle. They piled their boxed blooms on to a handcart. They'd been working in the field nearest the packing shed, so hadn't brought the tractor. The bell called again, and they rushed the cart over to the shed.

Vicki had hired a couple of local girls for the afternoon who would complete the packing and labelling, and make sure the flowers were ready to take to the island's tiny airstrip, and then on to the mainland markets.

They washed their hands at the sink in the shed. Matt still had a mutinous look that boded ill for the coming meal.

'I'm not hungry,' he protested, drying his hands.

'You will be when you see the food. Please don't upset Father today — for my sake, and Mother's.'

'All right. To please you, then, and Mother.' He smoothed down his lively blond waves.

Frederick Jamieson, a solid-looking man in his sixties, with a formidable air of authority was in the hall waiting for them. His thick hair, once the same strong colour as Vicki's, had faded to a distinguished silver, but his bushy eyebrows were still dark and forbidding.

He looked pointedly at the grandfather clock.

'Five minutes late, my dear — not a good example for Matthew.'

Vicki frowned. She admired and respected her father, but he had always been a difficult man to love. In his dealings with his children, he was often remote and aloof — except, of course, with Catriona. Vicki, however, was no longer over-awed by him. She was twenty-eight years old, and managed all the practical day-to-day running of the flower farm more or less single-handedly.

'Only a few minutes, Father.' She confronted him calmly. 'Conditions are perfect for picking. Matt's worked very hard all morning. We've been out since seven o'clock.'

'Well, don't delay any longer. Mother's put the meat on the table.'

There was an air of suppressed excitement about him, and for once he didn't comment on their unsuitable dress for Sunday lunch. Vicki had won that battle some time ago. There was no way she was going to change in the middle of a working day! Father had accepted it, but with ill grace. His dark suit, white shirt and sober tie were a silent reproach.

They usually ate in the big kitchen at the heart of the farmhouse, but Sunday lunch was served in the formal dining-room. This room was tacked on to the end of the house, like an afterthought, and was the farthest room from the kitchen! Fortunately, Vicki had persuaded her mother to invest in a hot-plate, so the food had some chance of keeping hot, and now the fragrant smell of roast beef persuaded Matt that he might be just a little hungry.

He took his seat at the long table, which could easily seat twenty people and seemed ridiculous for just four of them! He scowled at his father. Vicki nudged him.

'Smells good,' she said.

The room was her least favourite,

except at Christmas when a log fire lightened the atmosphere. Today, though, spring sunshine streamed in, and touched the polished mahogany surfaces with warmth.

'Where's Mother?' she asked, although she knew the answer.

'She'll be along. Just dishing up the vegetables. I'll carve now.'

From the distant kitchen they could hear clashing saucepans.

'Should I go and help?' Vicki half-rose from her seat.

'No, she can manage.'

In Frederick Jamieson's eyes, his wife could do no wrong. He had perpetuated the myth that she was a good cook — and however the Sunday lunch turned out, it had to be highly praised by all. Zoe Jamieson connived at the myth because she loved her husband more than life itself. It was her weekly penance and although she tried her best, the results were erratic.

Mr Jamieson lifted the savoury brown beef, surrounded by golden, crispy, feather-light puddings, from the hot-plate. This week, the meat was perfect. He began to carve.

His wife's entrance was dramatic. Pushing a trolley, rattling with dishes, she came in at top speed, flushed and breathless. Ten years younger than her husband, she looked far too youthful to have reached her early fifties. Her blonde curls, worn long and loose, were the same colour as her son's. Frederick despaired of his children's informal dress, but there was never a word of criticism for his wife. As an artist, she was allowed eccentricities! Today, her bright pantaloon trousers were topped by a long, Indian-cotton smock but as a concession to her one weekly domestic chore, an old-fashioned pina-fore flapped around her.

'Sorry, everyone — the potatoes gave me trouble, and I forgot the microwave was on defrost, so the carrots took an age. Vicki, you were out early this morning, and Matt, darling, you must be starving. Frederick, the gravy may be

15

cold, but the carrots . . . you see . . . '

She was starting to gabble but soon subsided, sat down, shook out a napkin, and beamed at them all, saying, as she did every Sunday lunch time, 'Well, isn't this lovely — the whole family together, except Catriona, of course.'

'And Aunt Cecily,' Matt interrupted, 'and why doesn't Steve come? He's practically part of the family.'

'He's busy on Sundays. It's the riding school's best day,' Vicki said. 'He often comes in the winter.'

'It's winter now but he hasn't been for weeks. It's so dull, just us.'

Matt ventured bravely, then jumped as his father rapped the table with the bone handle of his carving knife.

'That's enough, Matthew. Your mother has gone to a great deal of trouble to prepare the family dinner. I will not have you calling it dull. You should . . . '

'Frederick, don't.' Zoe's voice was low, but firm. Beneath her fey exterior, there was a vein of steel — she knew exactly how to handle her husband. 'Didn't you say you had news for us from your phone call before dinner?'

Mr Jamieson put the meat back on the hot-plate.

'Vicki, serve the vegetables, please. We'll enjoy your dinner first, Zoe, then I'll give you the news. It's an insult to your culinary skill not to give it full attention.'

Vicki caught her mother's eye and they exchanged smiles. Both knew that Vicki was by far the better cook, but they connived in preserving Frederick's fiction!

Meat and puddings were excellent, but the potatoes were decidedly charred and the gravy had a singed flavour. Nevertheless, the family did full justice to Zoe's efforts. Vicki collected up the dishes quickly, and hid Matt's concealed greens at the bottom of the four plates.

Zoe, duty done for this week, could return to painting her watercolours and charming the tourists into buying them.

She worked from a small studio in a barn conversion, and running the house and flower farm was an irrelevance to her. Vicki was much more practical in every way.

'The picking's nearly done then, Vicki?' Frederick spoke to his daughter, but watched his wife fondly as she quartered a fruit pie.

'All the flowers that are ready in the east field, yes. We should be finished an hour or so after lunch.'

'If you gave us a hand, Father, it would be even quicker. You don't come into the fields much now.'

Matt gave his father a sideways glance as both women rushed to intervene. Vicki was exasperated. Matt was pushing his luck — the sooner she got him back to the fields, the better!

'I'll have that pie later, Mother — Matt and I should be getting on,' she said.

At the same time Zoe pleaded, 'Can't you tell us your news now, Frederick?

Matt, go and make the coffee, please — it's all ready in the kitchen.'

'Finish your dessert first,' Frederick said. 'I doubt that you'd welcome my presence in the fields, Matthew. I worked hard enough there when I was your age — and well beyond. Just watch your tongue while you're under my roof.'

Vicki saw the light of battle flare in the young boy's eyes. Matt was growing up fast! Quickly she reinforced her mother's diversionary tactics.

'How much longer are you going to keep us in suspense, Father?'

Frederick wiped his mouth. The boy needed a good talking to, but he'd deal with Matthew later. What he had to tell them was much more important. He hugged the news to himself a few moments longer. Since the phone call, he'd thought of little else.

'Superb pie. Congratulations, my dear.' Zoe smiled. There was no point in telling him she had them delivered from the local baker!

'You may fetch coffee now, Matthew,' Frederick said.

He was stretching out the pleasure, anticipating his announcement. He watched silently as Matt wheeled out the debris, and brought in the coffee. Frederick waited until Zoe had poured four cups. With maddening slowness, he stirred a spoonful of sugar into his coffee.

'I have a family announcement.'

Matt's pained expression clearly said, 'For goodness' sake get on with it!' Vicki had been looking out of the window, watching the sun slide down the sky, hoping it would stay light long enough for a good gallop with Steve. She dragged her attention round to her father. What on earth could have brought such a smile to his face? All of a sudden, it dawned on her. Of course! She knew before he spoke. It had to happen sometime . . .

'I'm delighted to tell you that Catriona is coming home at last.'

His bombshell had the desired effect.

Zoe put down her coffee cup.

'That's wonderful. Why didn't you call me to the phone?'

'You were busy in the kitchen and I wanted it to be a surprise.'

'Yippee!' Matt's face had cleared. 'Action at last. Cat'll liven things up. When's she coming? Can I stay away from school?'

'Your sister's name is Catriona, and of course you can't take time off school. She thinks she'll arrive on Wednesday, so you'll see her during your half-term holiday. Vicki, we must get her room ready. Redecorate. New curtains . . .'

'How long a holiday has she?'

Vicki's brain was busy. It was two years since Catriona had been home, apart from a flying visit a year ago. Then she'd only stayed a few hours, pleading pressure of work. During most of the time, she'd been closeted with her father in his study, and Vicki had a shrewd suspicion that she'd come home to borrow money.

'It's not a holiday,' Frederick was

21

saying now. 'That's why it's such good news. She's coming home for good. Perhaps we ought to give her a new room, make a bed-sit for her — the large one overlooking the sea at the front, the one that used to be the playroom. She always loved it.'

So did I, Vicki thought, but you'd never let me have it. Now it was obvious he'd been saving it for his favourite daughter. He'd always hoped that Catriona would return to the island to live.

'If she's coming on Wednesday, there's no time to decorate. We're too busy on the farm.'

Vicki was trying hard to be objective. It would be great to see Cat. She would bring life to Piperidge. Her teenage years had been whirlwind, and she'd been far too wild for the island to hold her. She'd gone straight to London, where, after a spell as a photographic model, she was, by her own account, beginning to make it as an actress. Her last letter had been full of her latest offers, second female lead in a TV play, and a small part in a film to be shot in Los Angeles.

It was hard to believe that with all this excitement on offer, she would want to come back to the place that she'd so frequently referred to as 'Snoozeville.'

Frederick was looking put out and Zoe hurried to pour oil on troubled waters.

'Don't worry, Vicki. I'll help. We'll just do a clean-up of her old room for now. Splash out on a new duvet set maybe. We don't really know our daughter's taste any more, Frederick. Let's wait until she gets here. Don't forget, she's a woman of twenty-six now.'

'She won't have changed,' Frederick said confidently. 'She'll surely want to ride again — she always loved that. Vicki, when you go over to the stables for your ride, ask Steve about a horse for Catriona. It'll be our coming-home present.'

'But what's she going to do here?' Vicki's spirits were sinking even lower.

'She didn't say. Isn't it enough that she's coming home to stay?' Frederick finished his coffee and glanced at his watch. 'Perhaps you and Matt had better get on with the picking. Mustn't miss your ride. Steve will be so pleased Catriona's coming home.'

Vicki blinked. How could he be so tactless? Didn't he remember how Steve had felt when Catriona left the island, declaring she'd never come back?

Trying to keep the sarcasm out of her voice, she answered carefully.

'You're right, Father, I must make sure I have time off — with my fiancé. Don't expect me back for supper tonight. Come on, Matt. Back to work.'

Zoe put out a hand as Vicki went past, and gave her an understanding look. That and the sympathetic pressure on her arm told Vicki that at least somebody had not forgotten!

2

Matt, galvanished by the news of his other sister's imminent arrival, worked like a Trojan in the afternoon. The picking went so well that Vicki found herself with an hour to spare before her Sunday ride.

Whilst showering and changing into her jodhpurs, she faced the fact that she was feeling too antagonistic towards her father to want to stay in the house and be with him. Zoe, naturally, had gone back to her studio, lost in a world of her own as usual.

Vicki could have gone to the stables early and talked to Steve but it niggled her that she must be the one to tell him about Catriona's return to the island. How would he react? If he, too, showed the leaping excitement she'd seen in her father's and brother's eyes, the hurt would be almost more than she could bear.

So there was only one place to go — Aunt Cecily's cottage. There she had always been able to find a refuge and someone on whom she could rely to be on her side.

Cecily Jamieson was in her fifties now. Although she was reasonably well-off, she had chosen, after years of travelling, to come back to the island and live in a small, whitewashed house directly by the water. It suited her, she said, partly because of the proximity to her brother's family and partly because it gave her the chance to continue indulging her lifelong passion for sailing.

When Vicki reached the cottage, she found her unconventional aunt hard at work scraping away at a boat drawn up on her slipway. After one sharp glance at Vicki's face, she put the scraper down on the stone wall nearby.

'What's up?'

Vicki tried to laugh. 'Now why do

you think there's anything up? Am I so transparent?'

Cecily wiped her hands on a grimy rag. In her normal uniform of ancient dungarees and fisherman's smock, she was the antithesis of her more formal brother. It was hard to accept that they were so closely related — except for a certain high-cheeked patrician look they both shared, and the faded, dark-brown of her hair.

'Don't try to kid me that the wounded look on your face comes from nothing more than the horrors of Fred's Sunday lunch rigmarole. I know you too well,' she said.

It always had been impossible for Vicki to hide her feelings from this particular member of the family, so there didn't seem much point in not being honest now. Anyway, wasn't that what she'd come here for?

'You're right,' she said, 'there is something — but I'm ashamed of feeling so uptight about it. Father had a phone call from Cat. She's coming home — for good — and I'm all mixed up.'

It was a relief to admit the truth. Like going to confession and getting it off your chest, she thought, with an inward, wry amusement.

Cecily nodded.

'I see.'

Her bright, knowing glance held sympathy but it was not in her nature to show anything other than a brisk and practical attitude.

'I suppose everyone's gone completely over the top,' she said dryly, 'and will be treating her like the prodigal daughter.'

'Yes.' Vicki was filled with guilt at the sense of bitterness she recognised within herself. 'Not Mother so much,' she felt compelled to add. 'Just Father and Matt.'

Like a lot of slightly eccentric people, Cecily prided herself on calling a spade a spade.

'Zoe doesn't get excited about anything except her pretty paintings,' she said with brutal candour. 'That and keeping my bossy brother happy.'

'Oh, Cec, don't.' Vicki was driven to defend her parents. 'You shouldn't talk like that — especially when I know how fond you are of them both.'

'That may well be true,' her aunt conceded, 'but it's got nothing to do with the matter in hand. I'm neither blind nor stupid. You, my poor girl, have been carrying the weight of the farm on your shoulders for years. Fred on the other hand, for whom, as you say, I have a great deal of affection, can be both blind and stupid sometimes. He has never appreciated what you do. I've a jolly good mind to give him a piece of my mind. If ever a man needed a few home truths, he does!'

Vicki was horrified at the idea of a confrontation, on her account, between her formidable father and her redoubtable aunt.

'Please, don't, I couldn't bear it if you did.'

She was silent for a moment. Cecily

watched her, well aware of the girl's inward struggle. Finally she said brusquely, to hide her very real compassion, 'Well, come on, out with it. There's more, isn't there?'

'Yes.' Vicki took a deep breath. 'There's something else I'm worried about.'

Cecily's expression was inscrutable. Her eyes scanned the unhappy, tense look on Vicki's face, and her lips tightened.

'What we need is a cup of strong tea,' she announced, 'and we're going to sit in my kitchen and have a heart-to-heart. How does that sound?'

'Lovely.'

Vicki smiled gratefully and followed her aunt indoors. But once seated at the table in the sunny kitchen, she found it difficult to begin. Sipping from thick mugs, she tried to tell her aunt how she felt.

'I don't know what I would have done without having you to run to. Even when I was a child — when my puppy died — when I was upset — you were always ready to listen — be my confidante.'

Cecily's weather-beaten cheeks became even more suffused with colour.

'I should hope so, too. Everyone needs someone to run to once in a while. I'm just glad I was here. Now then, enough of that — what's bothering you? I'd like to hear it from you although I can guess.'

'Can you? That Steve might still be carrying a torch for Catriona? Do you suppose everyone will be remembering that? It's going to be too humiliating if the whole island is going to watch us together — and wonder. I thought, when we became engaged — well, he said it was all in the past and I believed him, because I wanted to. But now I don't know. It's bound to be difficult.'

'You're being illogical,' Cecily said firmly. 'If Steve had wanted Catriona that badly, he could have followed her to London. He didn't. In many ways she's a good enough girl but still a spoiled, selfish, little madam. I'll concede that she was fond of him, but the fact that she went away and hardly ever came back speaks volumes to me.

'They outgrew each other. I think you have to trust him when he says it's all in the past, for your sake and for his sake. Think about it rationally. If he were still in love with her, why would he become engaged to you of all people? Marrying her sister would mean being tied together as in-laws for the rest of their lives. He'd have to be a real masochist to be willing to see her again and again on that sort of basis.'

Vicki whispered, 'Well, we were thrown together — there aren't all that many girls my age on the island. And what you said, about being tied together, I wondered if that might be it — a way to still be connected to her.'

'Good grief!' Cecily exclaimed. She looked appalled. 'What on earth is wrong with you, my girl? Have you no self-esteem at all? I recommend you take a good, hard look in your mirror.

You're a smasher and it's about time you recognised it.'

'And of course you're not biased!' Vicki grinned, then grew serious again.

'I knew it was on the rebound when Steve first started asking me out. He'd adored Catriona ever since we were all kids. She liked him, too, but she was determined to get away — make her mark. She said everything on the island was boring — and that included Steve.'

'Was she right?' Cecily's look was searching.

'No, she was wrong.' Vicki's reply was vehement. 'He's lovely — and not at all boring. And he's become so handsome since he grew up. I'm so afraid that Cat will see him with new eyes now that he's changed and matured so much. Not only that, but maybe the old magic will still be there — for him anyway.'

'There you go again.' Her aunt sounded impatient. 'You're believing you won't have any say in the matter. Here you are, engaged to marry the man and you're afraid Catriona only has to crook her little finger to have him running back to her.'

'I just feel it isn't fair,' Vicki burst out. 'I never imagined for one moment that she'd ever choose to come back here permanently — that after her lifestyle in London, which she seems to love, she'd be willing to settle back to country living.'

Cecily sighed. 'Nobody ever promised that life would be fair. We didn't all have fairy godmothers doling out goodies at our christening, you know. As for coming back, I can testify that it's not all that easy getting away for good. When I was young, I couldn't wait to leave either — but the island pulls. It's like a magnet when your roots are here. You can never completely forget that it's your heritage. If you ever leave, you'll feel that, too.'

★ ★ ★

Ten minutes later, Vicki was on her way to her fiancé's stables, for her regular Sunday afternoon ride. This was another of Frederick's traditions but one she had no difficulty in agreeing to. As schoolgirls, both she and Catriona had been keen horsewomen and ridden several times a week. Since her father had failed to interest his wife or his son in riding, he had had to be content with his daughters' love of horses.

Far from being early, Vicki arrived fifteen minutes later than scheduled. It had been hard to leave the sympathetic presence of her aunt. But her father had always been a stickler for punctuality and it was ingrained that being on time was a courtesy to others. So, to make up the lapse, she had run the last few yards and was slightly breathless when Steve came out to meet her.

'I'm sorry, Steve. I stayed too long at Cecily's — we got talking.'

'Hi, sweetheart. Never mind, you're here now. I thought you were lost.'

He leaned down and kissed her lightly on the cheek, a crisp, masculine tang of horses and pine-scented after-shave emanating from him.

Vicki smiled at him. Smiling back at her from his six foot two, he was the epitome of the tweedy countryman — easy-going, good-humoured and good-looking. What more could any girl wish for than to be engaged to such a man? He was hardworking, too, and had made a success of the stables, already paying off his initial loan to the bank for converting his late father's farm into a different and more lucrative business. Gazing up at his tanned face, a pang of apprehension shot through her at the idea of losing him.

'Hey, you'll know me when you see me again.' Steve, in a characteristic gesture, ran a brawny hand through his hair. 'I feel like I'm being surveyed for market.'

'Sorry.'

Vicki tried to shake off her fearfulness. What would he say when she told him? She knew instinctively that it would be best to tell him straightaway, but she said nothing. What was the use of putting it off, she thought, angry at her own fears, but conscious also that she didn't want to risk shattering what they had, once and for all. Damn Catriona, she thought — whatever happens now, everything is smirched. She'd been possessed by the green-eyed monster and hated herself for it.

'Steve, could we take a few days away somewhere — just by ourselves?' she blurted out, almost without thinking.

He looked astonished, as well he might. Neither of them had ever considered such a thing before.

'Go away together? To the mainland you mean? This is a bit sudden, isn't it, Vicki? Frankly, I'd hesitate to leave the stables without a lot of planning — neither of the girls is capable of managing alone. In any case, you surely can't abandon the flowers at this time of year, can you? I thought you'd already started picking.'

Vicki looked crestfallen but she knew he was making sense.

'You're right. It was a silly idea. Forget it. Is Fleury ready for me?'

Steve looked relieved at the change of subject.

'She's been ready for ages. Raring to go.'

He called to one of the stable girls to bring out the mare, and the dainty-stepping horse was led across the yard, her hooves making a cheerful clip-clopping noise on the concrete.

'Thanks, Harriet.' Vicki took the reins and Fleury nuzzled an exploratory nose against her jacket. Vicki took from her pocket the lumps of sugar the animal had been expecting. 'Yes, you know I never forget don't you, my beauty,' she murmured.

'You spoil her,' Steve protested in mock reproval.

'She's worth it.' Vicki rubbed a hand lovingly up the mare's brown head.

'I'm on the new horse today,' Steve said, adding, 'She'll probably be a bit frisky, so I'll let you start off. The new mare is a great horse — a black called

Tamsin, but she isn't used to me yet. I may have to let her work off the fidgets a bit when we get started. So you and Fleury go at your own pace. We'll come back to join you, when I've calmed her down.'

'Right.'

Vicki put one foot into the left stirrup and submitted to Steve lifting her into the saddle. He grinned at her as he took firm hold of her slender waist and responded to the slightly anxious look she cast up at him by dropping a light kiss on her forehead. His lips were warm and reassuring. Then she was in the saddle and looking down at him.

Once again, as he put one muscular arm up to shade his eyes against the wintry sun, she thought how attractive he was. They were going to be married in less than a year's time — and had been engaged for a year already. Her fears were groundless. It was all right, of course it was.

Cecily, wisely, had said she should trust him and trust their relationship.

Otherwise what kind of life together could they expect? It would be absurd — and destructive — if Vicki were to be possessed by jealousy every time her sister was present — or even at any mention of her name.

Harriet had gone back in to fetch the new horse, Tamsin, for Steve. They were alone. Now was the time to speak.

Giving herself no chance for further hesitation, Vicki plunged into rather too casual speech.

'Incidentally, Steve, have you heard the news?' That was nonsense for a start. She knew he hadn't.

'News? What about?'

'Catriona. She's coming home.'

Steve had been tightening Fleury's girth and was having a little trouble with the buckle. Head down, he concentrated on what he was doing.

'Really? That's nice. Is she staying long?'

'Possibly for good, according to what Father says.'

When Steve looked up, his face was

devoid of expression. At least there was none of the instant ecstasy the family had exhibited, Vicki thought. Perhaps he was a little too blank though, had schooled his face muscles too carefully, in preparation for her scrutiny. She reproached herself for a suspicious mind.

The second sentence, however, had clearly surprised him, and he was making no effort to hide his amazement.

'Coming back to live? I don't believe it! She'll never last out.'

'Father seemed quite sure — he says would you find a horse for her.'

'A horse — for Catriona? Yes, of course, but it'll take a while to find the right one.' He appeared lost in thought. 'None of the tame mounts we use for lessons would do for Cat. We'd have to look for something with a bit of mettle.'

Tamsin had been brought out and was waiting for Steve to mount. She was certainly a handsome creature, black with a white star. As he climbed easily into the saddle, Steve said, almost to himself, 'I suppose she could ride Fleury until we find something a bit more spirited.'

The green-eyed monster was back on Vicki's shoulder. How could he be so crass as not to realise that what he had just said was insulting to her — and to Fleury. Her lovely Fleury — who was good enough for her, but suitable only as a stop-gap to her more tempestuous sister. It was galling in the extreme.

Steve was completely unaware of her mounting anger. He was, in any case, far too busy controlling Tamsin's desire to make for the distant skyline.

Unable to think of anything to say that would not sound like sour grapes, Vicki squeezed her thighs into Fleury's sides, tugged on the reins and the mare obligingly started forward. As she moved away, she heard Steve remind Harriet to prepare the big stallion in Stall Thirteen for Mr Jamieson's arrival, Frederick was probably already on his way to the stables, because he always arrived there precisely on the dot of four o'clock, just time to take his majestic canter before the light faded.

Steve had finally given Tamsin her head. They shot by Vicki and Fleury as they passed out of the open, white gate.

Well, let them go. She had no desire to ride at breakneck speed and, as Steve had said, they'd meet up again later. Vicki followed at a more sedate pace, determined not to let her happiest hour of the week be spoiled by her own doubts and fears. She was glad she'd got the telling over. At least she didn't have that to go through again.

Now she could enjoy the lovely, crisp, cold air, and the feeling of life reawakening again after a long winter. There was so much more greenery everywhere now, as far as the eye could see over the rolling downs. In the distance the sea was dark blue and white capped.

Steve didn't take long to return to

her and they rode together in amicable silence. He was enthusiastic about putting the new horse through her paces. Vicki, beginning to relax at last, told him about the early daffodil harvest. By mutual consent, neither of them referred again to Catriona.

As they were trotting back through the fields they spotted her father in the distance galloping towards a hedge and it was Steve who woke up to the fact that something was wrong.

'He's going too fast up to the gate!' he shouted.

Almost before the words were out of his mouth, he had spurred Tamsin into quick action and was heading towards the faraway figure. Vicki, slower to comprehend what was happening but following him nevertheless, was close enough to see her father fall but too far off to do anything about it.

The stallion, the biggest horse Steve owned, was not known as a jumper. But Frederick Jamieson, finding himself approaching the hedge at an unexpected speed, had made a last-minute decision to turn sideways and try to jump the gate. When the stallion resisted and stopped hard, at the last minute, he had tried and failed to wrench the horse in the other direction. Unbalanced by his efforts, he fell off and landed with a sickening thud. His daughter and prospective son-in-law could only watch helplessly. Steve reined in, leaped off and rushed to the groaning figure.

'Don't try to move. Where are you hurt?'

Frederick shook his head. Though fully conscious, he was too shaken to know very much. He closed his eyes in obvious pain as Vicki dashed anxiously to kneel beside him.

'Father, are you all right?'

Even in shock, Frederick still found this a regrettable question.

'No, of course I'm not.' He tried to turn his head. 'Where is the damn brute?'

Steve, who considered the accident had been human rather than animal error, held on to his temper.

'He's not far off. I'll get him later,' he said. 'Right now I'm going for help. Vicki, you'd better stay here until I get back.'

She nodded silently, and watched as he remounted and rode away. Frederick had not re-opened his eyes, but another groan escaped him.

Tentatively, Vicki took the slack right hand at his side and held it in her own. It felt strange to be holding her father's hand. She tried, and failed, to remember the last time she had done so. His body was twisted and his left shoulder held at a straight angle.

There was something weirdly uncomfortable in seeing her strong and dominant parent so vulnerable. It was unsettling to say the least — like an idol slipping off its pedestal.

He still said nothing and after a moment she came to the conclusion that he had fainted. She slipped off her jacket, folded it and laid it gently under his head. The air was becoming colder. She hoped it wouldn't be long before Steve brought help.

3

If ever a man was, by nature, a bad patient, it was Frederick Jamieson. He was stoical enough on the extremely uncomfortable trip to the small cottage hospital, across fields and lanes, keeping his teeth gritted and his eyes shut, but both nurses and doctors got their heads bitten off for their attempts to help him. Luckily, his irascible nature was well-known and nobody took much notice.

Once released, and ensconced in his bedroom at home, with his broken collarbone in a sling and his heavily-bruised body aching quite badly, he made sure no-one else was able to enjoy life either. Calling frequently for everything he wanted, short-tempered with nearly everyone, he took out his frustration and anger in sheer cussedness — mostly on Vicki because he never shouted at Zoe. In any case, the latter was in a considerable state of nervousness already.

After the accident, one glance at her mother's distraught face had persuaded Vicki to go in the ambulance with them. On seeing her beloved husband's pain and helplessness, Zoe had gone almost completely to pieces.

'Which was, of course, entirely predictable.' Cecily pronounced grimly, when she came up to the house next day and found Vicki coping with the demands of the invalid, the household and the continued running of the flower farm.

'She can't help it,' Matt said, defending his mother stoutly. 'She's just not like the rest of us. She sort of — doesn't live in the real world.'

Vicki smiled warmly. 'No, she doesn't, but thank goodness you do, Matt,' she said. 'He's been doing a tremendous lot for Father, Cecily — and comforting Mother as well. I couldn't manage without him.'

Cecily bestowed one of her rare smiles on her nephew.

'Good for you. Keep it up. I'll pop up every day and do whatever I can. Have you arranged for the cleaning lady to come in more often?'

'Yes, thank goodness.'

Vicki rubbed the heel of her hand against tired eyes. She had not had much sleep the night before. Her father had been in considerable discomfort and she had been kept busy looking after him.

'I'm off now,' Cecily said with her customary abruptness. Her face was set. It irked her that once again Vicki was overworked and under-appreciated. 'You know where I am, if you need me.'

'Yes, thanks.' Vicki managed a wan smile as she saw her off. 'At least we can be thankful that Cat doesn't arrive until Wednesday.'

Before the day was out, however, Vicki found that this particular blessing had been counted rather too soon! Matt, dutifully busy in the packing shed, rushed into the house during the afternoon.

'She's here.' His voice was jubilant. 'Come and see. There's a taxi coming up the lane.'

Vicki, hurriedly drying her hands on the kitchen towel, followed him outside, her heart sinking a little. Once again, so it seemed, Catriona had surprised them all. Well, that was in character. Without even trying to, she had always been a mistress of the unexpected!

As she waited by the gate, watching the old, black cab trundle towards them, Vicki's brain was busy with the problems of her sister's early arrival. There was a lot that would need to be done.

It would be useless expecting Catriona to be much help domestically. With the best will in the world, she was as hopeless in the kitchen as her mother. But at least she would cheer up her father and sit with him sometimes, which would take off some of the pressure.

As if arriving two days early were not enough, Catriona still had another little bombshell to drop on them. To Vicki's utter consternation, she had not come alone! As she stepped out of the car, looking ultra-sophisticated in a blue suit with a miniscule skirt which showed off slim, nylon-clad legs, someone else stepped out after her.

'Oh, no! I need an extra visitor like a hole in the head.'

Vicki was not aware she had spoken aloud. Luckily, Matt wasn't listening anyway.

The man accompanying Catriona was tall, lean and dark. After a quick glance around, he reached in to pay the driver and begin hauling out a pile of bags. Matt was oblivious to anything except the sight of his sister.

'Doesn't she look great?' He rushed forward and was first to reach her.

'Yes, she does,' Vicki murmured wearily, conscious of her own slightly bedraggled appearance. 'Great.'

Catriona, blonde hair gleaming and

golden earrings glittering, had the look, in the quiet, country lane, of an orchid blooming on a compost heap. She was as dazzling as the sun coming out after the storm. Wreathed in happy smiles, she was as thrilled to see her family as though they had been torn apart as refugees. Enveloping her brother in a scented hug, she let him go only to grab Vicki and do the same to her.

'Darlings, it's wonderful to see you. Oh, I can't believe I'm back. The island looks glorious, doesn't it, Zak?'

She half-turned to her companion, now well-burdened with a selection of feminine-looking luggage. He nodded but Catriona gave him little opportunity to express any views.

'Poor Zak. Wasn't it fantastic that he wanted to come, too? He's been carrying everything for me. But I had to bring such a lot now that I'm staying for good.'

She bestowed another wide smile on them all, entirely sure of her welcome, but Vicki's heart sank even more. It was true then. Father had been right — Cat did mean to come back and live here. And who was this man with her?

Her sister had remembered her manners now and was breezily introducing her companion.

'He's an old friend, and madly interested in sailing — as well as being the best photographer in the world. He's dying to start snapping around here. Seascapes and boats and birds and boring things like that. But he does people, too. All the best pictures of me were taken by Zak, weren't they, darling?'

Vicki looked with disfavour on the enigmatic-looking stranger who seemed quite prepared to be carried along in the train of her sister's enthusiasm. So that was the explanation for the two expensive-looking cameras. He had dropped the luggage again and was holding out his hand, first to Vicki, then to Matt.

In spite of his quietness, he carried an air of confidence. Dressed in casual though expensive-looking anorak, jeans and heavy sweater — clothes considerably more suitable to a ferry crossing than Catriona's — he still had an indefinable aura of town glamour.

He smiled at them both, saying quietly, 'Nice to meet you. Cat's been telling me a lot about you all — and the island. It sounded to me like an idyllic place.'

'It's the back of beyond,' Matt said cheerfully, adding grudgingly, 'I suppose it's OK sometimes.'

Then he picked up some of the bags and helped to carry them into the house. In a high, excited voice he began telling Catriona about their father's accident.

She was genuinely distressed and went straight upstairs, exclaiming with horror. Vicki could hear the emotional meeting with their father from downstairs where she and the stranger were left rather awkwardly facing each other. Catriona's voice, except when she bothered to lower it seductively, was the sort that could be heard easily at the back of a theatre.

'Poor, poor Daddy. What an absolutely dreadful thing to happen. I'm so glad I came home early.'

Nobody but Catriona ever called Frederick 'Daddy.' From her he not only tolerated it but even seemed to like it.

Vicki was wondering, rather worriedly, about the relationship between her sister and the man she had brought with her. Both of them gave the impression that they were accustomed to life in the fast lane. But island moral standards were still fairly old-fashioned.

Would Catriona expect to share a room with him? Surely not — she must guess that neither Zoe nor Frederick would be able to accept that. Or were they, really, just good friends? Oh, dear, having an outsider in the house was going to make life even harder than it already was — for all sorts of reasons, quite apart from the bedroom arrangements and having two extra mouths to feed.

Nonetheless Vicki was conscious of a lifting of the depression she had been feeling earlier. It was impossible not to enjoy the light-hearted presence of Catriona. Careless of other people's feelings she might be but already, just by being there — and being herself — she had managed to eradicate the oppressive air of the house. Even Matt, upstairs with her now, seemed like a different boy.

Vicki hugged to herself a secret, little pleasure, the only redeeming feature of the unwelcome stranger's arrival. How stupid she had been to get herself in such a stew about Steve's reaction to her sister's homecoming. Troublesome it might be, in some ways, but the fact that Catriona had brought a boyfriend with her was bound to make a difference. She wondered just how serious it was between them.

It had been so foolish of her to think of Steve as the lovesick schoolboy he had once been. He was her fiancé now and all of them knew it. As she stood, lost in thought, Vicki's face had been reflecting her feelings fairly obviously.

She woke up sharply to the fact that there had been a long silence — and that she was being watched. The stranger standing opposite her had been observing her varied expressions with a wry interest. There was a glint of humorous comprehension on his rather saturnine face and Vicki, feeling as though he knew exactly what was going on in her mind, flushed hotly.

'I'm sorry Mr — Mr . . . ' She floundered and was aware that he was watching her with an amused glint in his dark eyes. Had Catriona mentioned a surname? If so she couldn't remember what it was.

'Call me Zak.'

Totally perceptive to her embarrassment, he finally had the grace to change the subject and removed his intent look from her to their surroundings.

'Your house is fascinating. A positive museum piece. Nearly everything here would fetch a good price in an antique shop in London.'

Vicki was incensed. What dreadful arrogance! How dare he wander in from the metropolis, look down on them so condescendingly and kindly tell her that their possessions were saleable!

'It's been the family home for generations.' She injected into her voice as much coldness as she was capable of using. 'I hardly think any changes are likely to be made. We like it this way — my father prefers traditional things.'

Guiltily she pushed aside the niggling memory of how many times Frederick Jamieson's children, herself included, had pleaded for more modernising around their home. Never mind what they all said in the privacy of the family, it wasn't up to an uninvited newcomer to criticise.

He seemed to become aware of her frigid look.

'Sorry. That was rather tactless of me, I'm afraid. Believe me — I love antiques. It's just — forgive me if I'm being too blunt but I'd never have imagined this as the background for a girl like Catriona.'

Vicki had caught sight of herself in the mirror — dark hair tangled wildly, old jeans and sweater, even a patch of flour on her cheek. What a contrast to the vision upstairs.

'Really?' she snapped waspishly. 'I suppose you mean that her older sister, on the other hand, is eminently suited to this setting.'

She was sorry as soon as the words left her mouth. How ungracious! And how idiotic to show herself up so plainly. He would think her a jealous, stay-at-home, spinster sister.

The stranger's conciliatory expression had faded. Two lines appeared at the side of his mouth as his face hardened in surprise.

'Hey, what's this? I didn't say that — or mean anything like it.'

Vicki was instantly contrite. This was no way to behave to a guest.

'I know. I'm sorry — Zak. It's not your fault. It's just — I was up in the night a lot. I'm tired . . . '

There was no time to finish her apology. She was furious with herself and still angry with him, for having made it necessary. But Catriona was coming down the stairs again, looking gloomy.

'Isn't it awful? It seems all wrong to see Daddy laid so low.'

Then, with a mercurial change of mood, she flashed them both a dazzling smile.

'But it's so lovely to be here. The old place hasn't changed a bit.'

Vicki smiled back. It was impossible to think of Catriona, when she was present, as anything other than one of nature's children. She really meant it when she said she was upset about their father's accident, but as soon as he was out of sight, she could immediately throw herself into something else with enthusiasm and good spirits. In some ways she resembled Zoe very much.

Single-minded! A creature of the moment!

Now she seemed to have forgotten something, and put her hand to her mouth in contrition.

'Oh, Zak, I should have told you to get the taxi to wait, so that he can take you to the village to book into the hotel. We'll have to ring up for one.'

'No, please don't. I'd prefer to walk. I'll be glad to stretch my legs after the trip, and I'm quite interested in strolling about and having a look at things.'

He peered around at the piles of baggage and reached for a backpack.

'This is the only one that belongs to me.'

Vicki was ashamed of her over-whelming sense of relief that he was not, after all, expecting to sleep at the house.

She said hesitantly, 'I gather that means you're not staying with us?'

'Good gracious, no, that was never my intention.'

He leaned down and gave Catriona a light kiss.

'Enjoy being back in the bosom of your family. I'll ring you tomorrow once I've settled in.'

He turned and would have ambled off, except that Catriona, apparently not content with the quick peck, had put both arms around his neck and was gazing up into his face.

Vicki, an interested observer of the little scene, wondered if she should get back to her work in the kitchen but neither of them seemed to be bothered by her presence, so she shrugged and stayed where she was.

Catriona was at her most charming.

'Darling, it's been heavenly having you along on the trip — and I'm so looking forward to your being around for a while. In fact . . . '

She broke off and turned to Vicki, putting the pleading, little-girl tone into her voice that Vicki remembered of old. It was a tone that had always seemed to get Catriona exactly what she wanted — especially from her father!

'Do we have anything for dinner tonight that will stretch, Vicki? I expect you've got something tasty lined up. My sister,' she announced proudly to Zak, 'is practically a cordon bleu cook.'

Flattery will get you anywhere, Vicki thought cynically.

Nevertheless, her relief that he was not staying was tempered by regret at the way she had behaved. The least she could do was invite him to dinner, especially as Catriona had made it virtually impossible not to back up her invitation!

'It isn't anything very special,' she murmured, 'but I've been given lots of fresh mackerel. Do you like fish? There'd be plenty to go around.'

As invitations go, it was fairly tepid, and Zak seemed to have no difficulty in making a quick decision. Without hesitation he firmly refused.

'Thanks, but I'd really prefer to stay and eat wherever I book in tonight.'

'Just as you please.' Vicki accepted it

with composure and even Catriona only pouted a little.

'Party pooper,' she said with a roguish look up at him. 'But you must definitely come to dinner soon. You haven't lived until you've tasted Vicki's gooseberry soufflé.'

'I'll look forward to it.'

He nodded coolly and Vicki nodded back equally coolly. She heard him say, as Catriona walked outside with him, 'When I've found some decent restaurants or pubs I'll wine and dine you.'

'Lovely.' Catriona waved goodbye as he strode off, then turned and swept back to Vicki.

Alone for the first time, the sisters gazed at each other seriously. Catriona tilted her chin and flashed a dazzling smile, but Vicki was not deceived. She had seen that defiant tilt of the chin before and it always meant her sister was up to something. What was it this time, she wondered.

★ ★ ★

Cecily had packed in working on her boat for the day. The light wouldn't last much longer and she was longing for a hot bath. Gratefully she downed tools and stretched tired muscles. No fun, getting older, she reflected ruefully. A few short years ago she could have kept going for hours longer.

It was when she had cleared away her things and was standing at the kitchen sink, washing her hands, that she spotted the stranger. He was strolling along the path, gazing seaward, until he saw her boat, drawn up on the slipway. Instantly he straightened up, looked more alert, quickened his pace and came right up to it. To Cecily's annoyance he walked slowly around it, even putting out a hand to smooth down the side she had been working on.

Cecily wasted no time. It was unusual to see an unfamiliar human being, at least at this time of the year. There were often trippers and bird-watchers in the summer but seldom any strangers in the winter. Whoever he was though, he had no right to be poking about on her property. She marched straight out and accosted him.

'And who are you, I want to know?' she asked angrily.

The man was tall, with humorous, knowing eyes. He looked down at the aggressive but diminutive figure squaring up to him and grinned broadly.

'I'm nobody. Who are you?'

Cecily wanted to laugh at the unexpectedness of his reply but she wasn't going to let him get round her. Not that quickly anyway, though there was something about his smile that drew an answering response from her. She sternly curbed any tendency to smile back. He was out of order and she was going to let him know it.

She snapped sharply, 'Well, you may be nobody but I'm somebody. I'm the owner of this place and I'd like to know what you think you're doing, trespassing on it!'

'Yours is it? Then I tender you my

most abject apologies. As you will have gathered, I'm not a local — just here for a stay and looking around. When I saw this beauty I couldn't resist a closer look.'

He ran his hands once more over the sides of the craft and Cecily recognised at once that here was a fellow fanatic.

'You sail do you?'

'Not nearly often enough. But I'm hoping to remedy that now that I'm here.'

'Here? On the island you mean?'

'Yes, I arrived today. Do you know the Jamiesons?'

Cecily chuckled. 'Slightly.'

'I came from London with their daughter today.'

'Catriona?'

'Right first time. I've just come from meeting their son and their other daughter, who rather resembled a cactus plant.'

'What d'you mean by that?' Cecily, who had relaxed, bristled all over again, and Zak made haste to qualify his last observation.

'Sorry, I shouldn't have said that. I seem to have done nothing but apologise since arriving. Mostly because Vicki was as prickly as a hedgehog. But if they're close friends of yours, I'm quite ready to apologise all over again.'

Cecily considered. He seemed a tolerant sort of bloke so maybe he wasn't exaggerating. She could just imagine how Vicki had felt on having the two of them descend on her the very day after her father's accident.

'If you knew the situation there as well as I do, you'd understand,' Cecily said. 'The girl's got far too much on her plate — and if she thought you were going to stay, too, it was probably the last straw.'

'I see.'

Looking at him, Cecily decided that he probably did, too. For all his air of sophistication, there was a perceptive man under there, she decided. Not just worldly-wise but observant and shrewd, too. What on earth was a chap like this doing with an empty-head like Catriona, she wondered.

'It's been a pleasure meeting you,' he went on. 'I'm going to be around some time — taking photos.'

He indicated the cameras slung around him.

'It's my profession — but boats are my obsession. So I'm hoping to combine the two while I'm here.'

A new and very welcome thought had occurred to Cecily. If Cat had brought him, they must obviously be a twosome. And that was good news for the worries Vicki had had about Steve. Cecily was pleased. Vicki, in spite of being more intelligent and equally as pretty, had always had to come a bad second to Catriona. She had had little enough out of life so far, and Cecily would have hated to see Steve taken away from her as well.

A potential scheme to advance the throwing together of this rather pleasant townie and her younger niece occurred to her, though, if he were as keen on boats and sailing as he said he was, it would suit both their purposes.

Abrupt as ever, she said, 'Where are you planning to stay?'

He had picked up the backpack he had dropped on to the ground and was heaving it back on to his shoulders.

'I'm not sure yet. I guess there won't be that many hotels in the village here but it shouldn't be too difficult to find somewhere, should it?'

'No need.' Cecily, with characteristic impetuousness, had made up her mind. 'You can stay here. My spare room is large — and empty. Had an extra bathroom put on when I moved in, so you can have your own.'

'You're joking!'

Now she really had surprised him. He shook his head in disbelief. 'You don't even know my name — or how long I plan to stay — or anything. I could be Jack the Ripper — or on the run from the law.'

'Are you?'

He laughed. 'No. Catriona can give me a character reference if you want one. My name's Zak Cooper. I can't believe you've offered, but it would suit me wonderfully. But I'll only accept if you'll charge me the going rate.'

'No problem.' Cecily wasn't going to let a little thing like money sway her now. 'You can help me on the boats sometimes. And be my crew whenever I can take one out.'

'Fantastic.' Zak still looked thunder-struck at his luck.

He looked even more startled though when Cecily, showing him her large and sparsely-furnished spare room, casually mentioned that her name was Cecily Jamieson!

4

The warm spell continued and the spring flowers redoubled their efforts to come to precociously early bloom. Vicki felt as though she was on a treadmill moving far too fast ever to catch up. Taking advantage of her father's more mellow mood, she negotiated a modest wage increase for Matt and hired extra casual labour.

On Tuesday, the work force started at dawn. At first it was chilly, but the wintry sun was already shining strongly over the horizon's rim when Vicki called a halt for breakfast.

Coffee steamed fragrantly through the farmhouse, and led them down into the kitchen where Mrs Anne, a local woman who helped with the cleaning and cooking at busy times, had fried bacon and eggs while Zoe arranged the table. There was no sign of Catriona.

'She was still asleep when I looked in half an hour ago. No point in waking her after her long journey.' Zoe piled up the toast rack.

'When she does get up, maybe she could do a little light work in the fields. We could do with all the extra help we can get.'

It was hard for Vicki to keep any twinge of sarcasm out of her voice, and she was glad when her sister came into the kitchen, sleepy-eyed, yawning widely but full of eager willingness.

'Hi, everyone. I heard you, and I'd love to come out, Vicki. I feel like some fresh air. Give me a minute or two to dress.'

'We'll have breakfast first. And put on some warm things. It's still quite nippy out, although the sun's warming up.'

'No breakfast for me.' Catriona shuddered. 'Black coffee please, Mother. I never eat in the morning.'

'Don't know what you're missing,' Matt mumbled through a mouthful of sausages and bacon, his eyes lighting up at Cat's offer. The more the merrier out there, he thought, if they were going to get it done in good time.

'Are you sure you want to go out? You look half asleep still. We're not that pressed, and tomorrow will do.' Vicki's conscience pricked her.

'No — I must earn my keep.'

'No need to feel like that.' Zoe handed her a cup of coffee. 'You're allowed a little holiday.'

'Picking flowers by the sea is a holiday, after London.'

'But, I thought . . . ' Vicki stopped.

Her sister looked lacklustre, completely unlike her usual ebullient self. On her rare visits, she'd extended a glow of energetic well-being and happiness, which was quite missing this morning. Her hands trembled as she picked up her coffee cup, and after a small sip, she grimaced and set it down again.

'I'll go and get changed. Shan't be long.'

The gulls wheeled and squeaked over the stooped pickers.

'Cat's home,' Matt told them, tossing a piece of cold toast high in the air for the birds to squabble over. 'Now we'll have some fun.'

Already Father was in a much more approachable mood. Matt watched his sister's attempts to keep up with the others. Poor old thing, she was making a hash of it — out of practice. He'd give her a hand — she was only a quarter of the way down her row, and his was finished.

'Hey, Cat, I'll help . . . Cat.' His voice rose in alarm as she turned, swayed, put out a hand, and fell heavily on to the green stems. 'Vicki — quickly, over here.'

But Vicki had already seen and was by the prone girl in a flash, taking her wrist to feel her pulse. It was weak and fluttery, her arms very light. Cat had always been slender, but never this thin.

Beads of perspiration stood out on her forehead, but colour began edging back into the ashen face.

'Is she OK? What's wrong?' Matt leaned over anxiously.

'Just a faint, I think. She's not used to all the bending. It probably made her dizzy. And she had no breakfast, remember.'

Catriona opened her eyes. The ground beneath was rock hard, the bright blue sky an inverted bowl above. She remembered where she was — home on Tarlyon. Struggling upright, she put a hand on Matt's shoulder.

'Gosh, I'm sorry. Help me up, Matt. I — I must have slipped. What a fool.'

'You passed out,' Vicki said flatly.

'I'm fine now. I'll carry on.'

'You won't. We don't want another swathe of flowers crushed to death.'

'I'm sorry.'

'No, I'm sorry, that was meant as a joke, Cat. Matt, take her other arm and we'll get her indoors.'

By the time they reached the house, Catriona was walking unaided, and, though subdued, looked more or less her normal self.

'I tell you, I'm all right now. Let's go back.'

'We'll have coffee.' Vicki was firm.

At the front door, Zoe met them, painting gear under her arm.

'Catriona, what is it? I thought you ought not to go out today.'

'Please, don't fuss, Mother. It was just a dizzy spell. The air's so good here, I expect my lungs have had a shock. Probably missing the toxic fumes of Oxford Circus. I'm just sorry I've held up the workers.'

Vicki had put on the kettle. 'It's a good excuse for a break.'

A door across the hall opened and Frederick Jamieson, in plaid wool dressing-gown, and resting heavily on his stick, stood in the entrance.

'Father! What on earth are you doing? You should be in bed. The last thing we need is another crock.' Vicki rushed to help him.

'Don't refer to me as a crock, please. I'm getting up. I can walk quite easily.' His wince of pain belied his words, but he clumped into the kitchen and sat down by the table. 'You're in early. What's wrong?'

Catriona went over to him, and he took her hand.

'My fault. I guess I'm not used to hard labour. I felt a bit dizzy, so Vicki called a coffee break.'

'Dizzy?'

'I'm all right now — honestly. Fit to pick an acre.'

He sighed. 'What a home-coming for you. Not how I'd planned it but never mind, we'll go ahead with your welcome-home dinner tonight. Vicki, you've got everything laid on? I should have got the wine up from the cellar last night, but maybe you could run and get it now. It's your birth year, Catriona. You did remember to invite Cecily, Vicki — and I do hope you haven't forgotten to phone the bulb suppliers.'

'Father!'

The exclamation stopped him in mid-flow. Vicki's exasperation had made her uncharacteristically shrill. But the last demand was the last straw — the bulb suppliers had always been his particular area. Her aunt's words had been that he needed a few home truths! Well, perhaps she wouldn't go that far, but it was time to make a stand.

'Do you realise just how much I still have to do to get the flowers to market? A dinner party I can do without! I'm as pleased as you are that Catriona's home, but couldn't we postpone the grand celebration until the work's done?'

There was an astonished silence. Rebellion from this quarter was quite unexpected. Frederick's mouth was set in a stubborn line.

'I can't believe I'm hearing this. What is wrong with you, Vicki? Surely a meal for your sister isn't beyond you? We have to eat anyway, and a few extra touches wouldn't take too much.'

'In the dining-room? Family silver? Best napkins? Flowers? Crystal? Five courses? I'm sorry, Father, but it's just not on. Not for me.'

With apparent calm, she took a long drink of coffee, but inwardly she couldn't help a tremor, in spite of her twenty-eight years. It was ridiculous, but she couldn't ever remember defying her father so openly.

Catriona broke the silence. 'I don't want . . . '

Her mother, always the peacemaker, was quick to intervene.

'Vicki's right. She's had a lot to do lately.' Her husband started to speak, but she hurried on. 'You're right, too, dear — we must mark the occasion, but it won't be left to Vicki. Matthew is quite old enough to deal with the wine, and Annie and I will arrange a little buffet. We'll have a dinner party after the flower harvest. I'll ring Cecily now. And how about your friend, Catriona? We'll ask him, too.'

'It's a family affair,' Frederick protested, just as Matt nodded towards the window.

'He's outside now,' Matt said, getting to his feet.

'He won't want to come,' Vicki said, her outburst subsiding as quickly as it had erupted.

'Of course he must come.' Zoe was firm. 'He'll be the special quest. Vicki, you need a break. Go over to Steve's and take Fleury out. Off you go — I insist.'

Her mother insisting on anything was so unusual that Vicki did as she was told without a murmur.

Ten minutes later, in jodphurs and jacket, she came downstairs, in much better spirits. She was a little ashamed of her outburst, but she didn't regret it. It was about time she staged a revolution.

The atmosphere in the kitchen had lightened. Catriona, flushed and animated, perched on the arm of her father's chair. Zak was showing Matt the intricacies of a very high-tech camera, the boy handling it with awed respect. Vicki had passed her mother in the hall, discreetly phoning an emergency order to the local baker. As Vicki so often suspected, Zoe was capable of rising to any occasion if she chose to! Vicki went over to Catriona.

'Sorry about that, sis! It had absolutely nothing to do with you. It's lovely to have you back.'

'Don't apologise. It was all my fault. I feel great now. Why don't we all come over to the stables with you? I'd love to see Steve. Zak, you should meet Vicki's fiancé. He'll be at the party tonight, too, though he doesn't know it yet. Has he changed much, Vicki?'

'I suppose he has, since you went away. He was more your friend than mine then. You know he went to America after you left. He came back a couple of years ago, and started the riding school. That's when I got to know him again.'

'He came back, too.' Catriona sighed.

'It seems, Zak, that everyone does in the end.' The eagerness in her eyes died for a moment, then she said, 'Steve and Vicki had been engaged for a year.'

'That's nice. Congratulations. Is the wedding soon?'

'Late summer, we think, to fit in with the businesses — the flowers and the riding school. Look, are you sure you want to come? Steve may be busy and I shan't be long — I can't spare too much time . . . '

'You go and stay as long as you like.' Matt, with a sudden deep voice of adult authority, startled them. 'I'll make sure Jen and Kay keep at it, too.' His take-over bid caused nearly as much of a stir as Vicki's earlier outburst.

She accepted gratefully. 'Thanks, Matt. See you later then. Father, if there's to be a party tonight, you'd better rest now. Everything seems to be under control.'

As they trooped out, she exchanged a conspiratorial wink with her young brother as they headed towards the Land-Rover.

Catriona drove, bumping them along the tracks like a racing driver.

'Much more fun than London driving,' she announced as they drew into the stable yard. Vicki looked at her anxiously. There was a frenetic air about her, as though compensating for the morning's langour.

Harriet looked surprised to see them.

'Are you all riding?' she asked, eyeing Zak with interest.

'I'll take Fleury out, if you'll get her ready, but we'll see Steve first,' Vicki replied.

'OK. He's in the house. Looks as though he saw you coming.'

She jerked her head towards the low, stone cottage, in which Steve and Vicki were to live after the wedding. He was already on the doorstep, hair wet and tousled, bare, muscular legs showing below a thick towelling bath-robe.

'I saw you from upstairs. I was in the shower.'

His smile was wide and welcoming, as he kissed Vicki. Then he looked at Catriona. She reached up and put her hands on his shoulders.

'Steve, you're taller than I remember — and broader. It's great to see you.'

Vicki watched her fiancé. His eyes were alight with affectionate friendliness as he returned the embrace.

'You're very thin, Cat. Hectic London life?'

'You could say so. This is my friend, Zak Cooper.'

'Welcome to Tarlyon, Zak. How long are you here for?' The two men shook hands.

'I'm not sure. I'm enjoying looking around. I may stay for a while.'

'Guess what? He's put up at Aunt Cecily's,' Cat said, with a giggle. 'I can't imagine what they'll have to talk about.'

Steve remembered his duties as a host.

'Don't stand on the doorstep. Come in — I've got coffee on.'

'But you didn't know we were

coming — unless Father phoned.' Vicki frowned.

'I'd like to pretend it was second sight, but yes, he did. That's why I was in the shower. Sorry the place is in such a mess,' he apologised, as he led them into a square, beamed kitchen with a half-stable door. 'The builders have abandoned us and Vicki and I never seem to have the time . . . '

'It'll be great when it's done.' Catriona wandered round the room. 'A mix of old and new.'

'Very space-age high tech.' Zak looked at the modern cooker and butcher's table in the centre of the room.

Steve spoke defensively. 'We're both going to be working after we're married, so we need to be streamlined.' He took milk from a large, built-in fridge.

Vicki recognised the tense set of his shoulders, and reached to take mugs from the hooks.

'I couldn't agree more.' She squeezed

his arm. 'Harriet's saddling up Fleury. Just for an hour.'

He smiled down at her, then turned to Catriona. 'You, too? Your father asked me to look out for a horse for you. I've got just the mare — on trial.'

'I'm out of practice. I'll leave it a while. Zak rides.'

'Not today I don't. I'm tempted, but maybe I can fix it another day. I promised Cecily I'd go sailing this afternoon so I ought to go. I'll walk back. How about you, Cat?'

'No, I'll stay and look around. I'll be fascinated to see what Steve's done to the stables. We've got a lot of catching up to do.'

'Can't you ride with me, Steve?' Vicki asked.

'I'd love to, but I've a couple of new pupils in half an hour. The start of the tourist season.'

'Business is obviously doing well,' Zak murmured politely, draining his coffee.

'You can find your own way back?' Cat asked him.

He touched her hair gently, saying laughingly. 'I think I can manage. It's a small island. I'll enjoy the walk and I've got my camera. See you later at the party.'

'Party?' Steve looked enquiringly at Vicki.

'Didn't Father mention it? He wants a welcome-home supper for Cat. You'll come?'

'Of course. Now I must go and dress. Look around the stables, Cat. Harriet will show you the new mare.'

'I'll stay here and wait for you. I'd like to see the rest of the cottage. It's going to be lovely.'

'We think so,' Vicki said icily before she went out to mount Fleury.

★ ★ ★

By evening, Zoe and Annie had worked a small mircale. As a concession to Mr Jamieson, food was set out in the dining-room, where candles and a log fire gave an intimate elegance.

'It's lovely, Mother.' Vicki, dressed in an ankle-length skirt and silk top, hugged Zoe. 'You're a marvel.'

'It wasn't very difficult. Matt helped, and Annie. Frederick does so love these occasions.'

'How is he?'

'Fine. He had a sleep this afternoon, while you were out picking. He'll be along for a final check.'

'Hard to fault anything here. Not that he ever does — with you.'

Vicki looked hungrily at the enticing spread. A centrepiece of cold fresh salmon was flanked by mini savoury pies and open sandwiches. Pottery bowls of trifle and fresh fruit salad balanced the savouries, while decanter and crystal glasses winked at the candles.

Zoe, formal in peacock blue silk, had piled her pale hair up high. 'Yes, I'm lucky.'

Vicki hugged her. 'I think you're

wonderful, and I love you.' She kissed her mother on the cheek.

'Goodness, Vicki, perhaps I should do this more often.' Zoe laughed, returning her hug. 'You're usually so undemonstrative. Now I must go and see if your father's ready.'

The party was soon well under way. Frederick, centrally placed, was in good humour. This was how he'd always imagined it — surrounded by his family, looking towards a secure future. There was no need for any of them ever to leave the island again. The Jamieson flower farm would continue to thrive down the generations. There'd always be a market for fresh flowers. Just so long as it was kept in the family.

He eyed the company speculatively. Even Matthew looked respectable in trousers and shirt. No tie but at least he'd made an effort! Steve and Vicki make a splendid couple. Steve's strength would be useful in the coming years as his own declined. Zak Cooper, the fellow from London was an unknown quantity, but if he made Catriona happy ... The fellow was reading the labels on Catriona's special wine. It was time for a toast. With some difficulty he'd decanted the precious Bordeaux that morning. He adjusted the sling on his left arm.

Zak saw him struggle to his feet and pick up the heavy glass decanter.

'Can I help, sir?'

The older man frowned. Part of the pleasure would be to pour the precious liquid into the glasses — but one-handed? If it slipped ...

At last, he asked gruffly, 'Could you pour the wine?'

'Superb vintage,' Zak commented. 'A first growth, too.'

Frederick warmed to Zak's appreciation. No-one else in the house was in the least interested in his wine cellar. It would be nice to have a wine buff in the family.

'It's the year Catriona was born. I laid it down specially, and fortunately it was a great vintage.' They both sniffed the wine appreciatively. 'Fantastic bou-quet.'

Frederick's voice then cut across the general conversation.

'Everyone — please. I'd like you to toast our prodigal daughter with this, her special wine. Catriona — you first.' He handed her a goblet.

'Not for me, thanks. Red wine's a bit heavy and I've already had some cider.'

She was flushed and wide-eyed, her blonde hair hanging loosely round her shoulders. Her father's face registered dismay to a comical degree.

'But it's for you. It always has been — all your life it's been waiting. You must have some.'

'I don't like red wine. I never have done.' Then, as his face dropped even more, she took the glass from him. Oh, well, a sip wouldn't hurt! It was worth it to see the gratified look on his face.

Zak and Matt passed round the glasses, and Frederick went into his prepared speech of welcome. It was fulsome, and Catriona sipped her wine again. It was quite pleasant really, the taste full and fruity. Perhaps she could get to like it. She sipped again — and again, her control beginning to slip away.

Zak, savouring the fine claret, watched her. It was very alcoholic, and shouldn't be gulped as Catriona was gulping it.

'Steady,' he said to her very quietly.

Cecily, her eyes on Vicki, heard him. She wished Frederick wouldn't be so embarrassingly flowery about Cat. It didn't do Vicki's self-esteem any good at all. She wondered irritably if her brother would ever stop speaking as though he was addressing a public meeting of Victorian elders.

' . . . so our lovely daughter has returned to the welcoming bosom of her family, and I can't sufficiently express our delight that she has finally decided to come back to Tarlyon — this time, for good.'

Catriona blinked. Her head felt fearfully muzzy. Had she come back for good? And why had she come back? Memory trickled back. Of course. Well, they may as well know now. She hadn't intended a public announcement, but what difference did it make? They might as well know now. Everyone was here — it would save the bother of spreading the news later.

'Father,' she interrupted, 'I'm not sure about for good. You see, my future plans are uncertain.'

Frederick frowned. He wasn't quite finished.

' . . . but I need time, away from London,' Cat went on. 'You see, I'm going to have a baby. That's why I'm here.'

Frederick clutched the edge of the table with his good hand.

'Oh, no!' He sank heavily into his seat, and Zoe flew to his side, bending down to comfort him. He groaned and Vicki thought she heard him murmur, 'Not again,' but she couldn't be sure.

5

In the stunned silence which followed Catriona's announcement, Frederick seemed to have aged ten years. Nobody spoke. They all watched him, with varying degrees of apprehension. At first he shook his head slowly, in denial, unwilling to acknowledge, or accept, the unpleasant detail of his favourite daughter's condition.

Catriona, for all her bravado, had a frightened look about the eyes. Vicki, feeling sorry for her, was moved to go over and put her arm around the thin shoulders. Since Frederick had not spoken she decided to be the first to say something — and was determined that it should be something compassionate and positive.

'Well, Cat, if you're going to have a baby, thank goodness you've come home. It's by far the best place to be when you need looking after.'

Cecily, who was known to be ascerbic and frequently had little patience with Catriona, was uncharacteristically quick to back up Vicki.

'Yes, it's at times like this that you need your family,' she said, looking meaningfully at Frederick.

But he was lost to anything but his own pain. They had all looked at Frederick and one by one, they'd been forced to look away again. So much naked hurt on a face was hard to take.

Catriona, whose sophistication had dropped off her like a discarded cloak, said, in a little-girl-lost voice, 'Well, I thought that, too. But not if you're going to throw me out into the cold, cold snow, Daddy.'

Her giggle and the flippancy was a thinly-disguised fearfulness but still her father said nothing. He had covered his face with his good hand, in order to hide from their sympathy.

Matt, uncomfortable, yet excited with the atmosphere of heavy drama, rushed in where angels fear to tread.

'Gosh, you mean I'm going to be an uncle? But who's the father, Cat? Are you going to marry him?'

It was the question everyone wanted to know the answer to; and no-one had had the courage to ask!

Zak had been standing slightly back from the family circle. Now everyone except Frederick and Catriona, whose gazes had locked, turned and stared accusingly at him. In the same moment, Zak became aware of what they were all thinking. He looked startled and held up both his hands as though to fend something off.

'Now wait a minute . . . I . . . '

'What a way to meet the family,' Vicki said scathingly.

He looked straight at her and said gravely, 'Catriona asked me to come with her. She wanted . . . '

'Daddy, please don't look at me like that,' Catriona burst out with a sob in her voice, unaware of the confrontation behind her. 'I know I've been stupid but it isn't all bad. At least I want to keep the baby. I mean to bring it up myself. You wouldn't have wanted me to do anything else, would you?'

Zoe was still kneeling by her husband and she spoke for both of them.

'No, of course we wouldn't. And we'll help all we can. But it's all such a big shock. You must give your father time . . . '

Catriona's face crumpled. 'I'm sorry, I'm so sorry to have let you down.'

Frederick had never been able to bear Catriona's tears. At last he spoke, rousing himself from the torpor of shock and crushed hopes to say heavily, 'I can't pretend I'm not horrified. But we love you and that's all that matters.'

He held out his good arm for her to come and embrace him. Catriona rushed forward and hurled herself on to his chest, a move which, from the wince he gave, obviously caused him quite a deal of pain. Zoe put an arm around each of them, an expression of infinite relief on her face.

Vicki knew then, with a sense of thankfulness, that her father, hard and rigid as he sometimes was, still loved his family more than anything else. She was ashamed of a sneaking belief that it would all have been different had it been her. She could imagine him doing a never-darken-my-doorstep-again act had it been his elder daughter who had come home with such news. But, no, that wasn't fair. She was only speculating on a hypothetical question, so why torment herself?

But there was still the problem of Zak Cooper. Turning back to him, Vicki said boldly, 'I'd like to know what you mean to do about this.'

Catriona stood up. With one of her mercurial changes of mood, she seemed to have returned effortlessly to her usual light-hearted self.

'Zak? Why should he have to do anything about it?'

'Well, isn't he . . . oh, no!'

Vicki suddenly felt rather silly. She had jumped to the first conclusion which seemed likely. But she knew she was not the only member of the family to have assumed a relationship between the photographer and her sister. And now she was supported by Steve who had been looking thoroughly unhappy at being in the middle of such a private family matter.

'You can't blame us for thinking you're the father,' he said in their defence. 'If you come together to the island like this, is it any wonder?'

'No.' Zak's deep voice, by contrast, was calm and serene. 'I don't blame you at all. But I think you'd better tell them the truth, Catriona.'

'I have told them the truth.' She was indignant. 'Zak came because he was interested in photographing here. He's producing a book and wanted to have time to take pictures of birds and seascapes — and to go sailing. He knew about my problem. I had to confide in someone and it was really sweet of him to be company for me.'

She smiled sunnily at them all,

convinced that, now the news was broken, everything could quickly go back to normal. So they were all wrong about Cartiona's London friend. They had put two and two together and made it five. Before courage had time to fail, Vicki turned to Zak and said quickly, 'It seems I made a mistake. I owe you an apology.'

Zak smiled at her. 'It was natural enough. In other circumstances I might have thought the same.'

Zoe said, 'Well, if Zak is not the father of your child, darling, then who is?'

Catriona looked secretive, and stubborn.

'It doesn't matter who he is. We've agreed to part for ever and that's the way we both want it. This will be my child and nothing to do with him. He doesn't come into it. As for who he is, I've promised I'm not telling — ever.'

Once again everyone in the room was stunned into silence. But the effect of this defiant statement was more than

Frederick was prepared to bear. He rose with difficulty and left the room without another word. Zoe followed, leaving Cecily to break the silence.

'You've certainly put the cat among the pigeons this time,' she said dryly.

Not surprisingly, Matthew was the only one who dared to laugh!

★　★　★

The revelations of the night affected them all, and a pall of unease hung about the place for days. But the life of the flower farm had to continue. They were so busy cutting and packing that Vicki found the daylight hours too short to get everything done. For the first time, she even cancelled her Sunday ride.

Catriona made no more attempts to help with the picking. Instead she seemed bent on making herself scarce and was seldom there, not even in the kitchen, when the pickers came in for their coffee break. She did return one day whilst they were still there and seemed disconcerted at the presence of her sister.

'Oh — I thought you'd be back in the fields.'

'No, we came in later today.' Vicki gave her a level look. 'Does it matter? Are you trying to avoid me?'

'Don't be silly. Why should I do that?'

Catriona, with an airy nonchalance, went to the stove and poured herself a cup of coffee, but Vicki was not deceived.

'Look, Cat, you don't have to feel guilty because you're not doing anything. We — I — don't expect you to, now that we know . . .'

She remembered the others in the kitchen and stopped short, finishing lamely, 'Anyway, nobody expects you to work in the fields.'

Instead of looking cheered by what Vicki said, Catriona looked as though she wanted to cry.

'It isn't . . . ' she began, then shook her head as though uncertain how to carry on. 'Have you seen that strange, old man?' she asked suddenly, in an obvious attempt to change the subject. 'I've been going on — walks — and I've seen him twice, once in the back of the island taxi. He always seems to be looking around here.'

'What a cheek!' Matt came in on their conversation. 'Perhaps he's a secret agent.'

Vicki took his empty cup from him and put it firmly on the table.

'Even if the whole place is over-run with secret agents, we haven't time to do anything about it. We have to get back to work.'

'OK.' Matt shrugged philosophically, but he gave Catriona a conspiratorial wink. 'It's terrible having such a slave-driver for a sister,' he said cheekily.

Catriona smiled back at him but after they had gone, she continued to gaze after them. The troubled look on her face was so apparent that when Zoe came into the kitchen, she was moved to take her hands and say soothingly, 'It's going to be all right, darling. Don't worry about the baby. We'll manage, when the time comes — we've told you that.'

'Oh, Mother, you don't understand.' Catriona stood up restlessly with a sigh of discontent. 'It just seems to me that nothing is ever simple any more.'

'Nothing ever was simple, Cat,' Zoe said, quite sharply for her. 'I'm afraid we did you a disservice if we brought you up to believe that life was going to be all plain sailing. Did we do that, I wonder. Have your father and I taught you that if you want a thing you must have it? Is that it?'

'I don't know what you mean.' Catriona's cheeks were a wild rose colour, and her eyes slid away from her mother's gaze.

'Don't you?' Zoe asked. 'Don't you really? Then there's no more to be said, is there? But I wouldn't like you to think that anything comes without a price. Or that someone else is always going to pay it.'

Out in the fields, Vicki had been pleasantly surprised by the arrival of unpaid help! Zak had lounged up as they settled back to their picking and asked if he would be in the way if he first watched for a while and then joined in.

'You're very welcome,' she said. 'But don't you have lots of things you want to be taking photos of?'

'I've got quite a portfolio already. And don't think I'd be doing it for nothing. I want permission to take pictures as well.'

'Of picking?'

'Of you picking.'

'Oh.' Vicki didn't know whether to be flattered or annoyed. 'Why me particularly?'

'Your colouring partly — against the green, and the sky, that shiny, dark head of yours is great.' He grinned. 'And although you may not know it, you do it with a peculiarly lithe movement that I hope to capture — very graceful.'

'Thanks.'

Deciding that, although a little embarrassed now, she had every right to be flattered after that, Vicki bent to her task again, explaining the best way as she went.

'You take the cutters so — and cut sharply and cleanly here, then lay them so. It's really easy but you have to get into a swing. Now you try.'

Zak did. His efforts were painfully slow at first but he took very little time to grasp the best technique and within another fifteen minutes he seemed to be as efficient as anyone. Once Vicki saw that he could be trusted to get on alone, she went to an adjacent row.

They worked in companionable silence until both began to be aware of a change in the air, and of the wind rising. The sky began to darken and they both stood up and looked around. Everyone else was doing the same. Matt and the two girls were looking upward at the threatening black clouds rolling in off the sea.

'Hey, Vicki, that looks like a storm coming,' Matt yelled across at her unnecessarily.

Vicki's heart was sinking. This was what she had feared most — and the weather forecast had not been good. That was part of the reason they'd been working with such maniacal energy lately.

Already, in just a few minutes, the atmosphere had become damp laden. And all the flower farms in this part of the world knew that storms could come with devastating suddenness and ferocity.

She called out to everyone, 'I'm sorry if it is a storm, but we must carry on as long as we can — and get as much as possible inside. A bad storm can flatten the rest of the harvest.'

They all returned to the job with a renewed sense of urgency but nobody could completely ignore the rain when it came — or the increasing velocity of the wind. Zak looked at Vicki.

'Do we go on?' He had to shout over

the sound of the gale. She looked at him pleadingly. 'Please. Some of it will be ruined. We must save as much as we can.'

Matt and the others had recognised that already. None of them had made any attempt to stop and were gathering, packing and carting as fast as the conditions would let them.

Another figure had appeared at the edge of the field. It was Cecily, swathed in an elderly anorak and wellington boots.

'Tell me what to do!' she shouted.

'Thanks.' Vicki gave her a grateful smile. 'Could you help take the cartloads to the packing shed? Get them under cover.'

Always a woman of few words, Cecily simply nodded and got on with it. The rain was heavy now but nobody complained. With the water running down their faces they simply shook it off, gritted their teeth and carried on.

Vicki was feeling bitter. Here they were, just into March, with an early

Easter coming and this had to happen. It was absolutely vital to get the bulk of the flowers packed before too many were battered. She let nothing of what she felt show, however. Nothing must get in the way of the operation. Down, clip, lift, load, on and on they went like automatons.

When she got to the end of the row, Zak was almost level with her. She smiled gratefully but was too breathless to say anything. Then they saw him! A struggling, heavy-breathing Frederick appeared in the path between the fields, fighting hard not just to stay upright but to push one of the loaded carts.

'Father!' Vicki screamed at him. She ran forward. 'Go indoors! You must be mad to have come out!'

He looked too spent even to protest. She had no idea how long he'd been there. Already his head was darkened and drenched by rain and sweat. 'Got to help,' he gasped. 'Need everyone.'

Vicki was too angry with him even to

try to be tactful. She yelled forcefully, 'That's rubbish. All you're doing is making it harder for everyone else. Go in, now!'

Zoe had seen, too. She came rushing up, wearing a waterproof and sou'-wester too big for her. She grasped her husband by his good arm and began pulling him back to the house, scolding all the way.

'Oh, you stupid man, you're wet through. I'm going to put you straight to bed. And we'll be lucky if you don't catch pneumonia. How could you, darling, how could you?'

Like a tame bear, Frederick allowed her to lead him away and the final view Vicki had of her father was the hangdog look he cast back at her, as though deeply ashamed of his own incapacity.

She could only be relieved that someone had the power to overcome the stubborn, dogged spirit that had made him come out in the first place.

There was no time to worry further

about him though. They must go on. Wearily she pushed the wet hair out of her eyes and bent to her task. She was unable to supress a chuckle as she recalled what Zak had said — that her shiny dark head looked good and she worked with grace. Well, that was certainly nothing like the reality now. She must look like an ancient peasant woman!

Five minutes later, the rain ceased abruptly and the wind dropped. The storm had moved on as rapidly as it had arrived. All of them were soaked and aching by then but as they stood and looked up at a watery sun appearing, Matt led them in a rousing cheer of thankfulness. Vicki beckoned everyone around her.

'Cups of coffee and a change of clothes for everyone up at the house,' she said, and gave them each a hug of heartfelt gratitude before following them.

Zak fell in beside her. His black hair had gone into tight curls.

'You all have my admiration.' His dark eyes showed that he really meant what he said and Vicki laughed, conscious of her drenched appearance.

'I can't imagine what for,' she said. 'I must look like a drowned rat. But I really appreciate the way you muscled in and worked so hard under those awful conditions. Thank you.'

She held out her hand as she spoke but Zak ignored it and, to her surprise, put his arms about her. He said lightly, 'Everyone else merited a hug so I'm not going to be left out.'

After a little hesitation, Vicki put her arms about him and returned the pressure. She said warmly, 'No indeed. I'm sorry I left you out.'

Their clothes were so soaked that the contact made squelching noises which reduced them both to laughter. Looking at his amused face so close to her own, Vicki wondered how on earth she had ever thought him an aloof and critical townie. Today he had shown himself in a very different light.

He's a nice man, she thought — and just the sort you need to have around at a time of crisis.

6

Vicki's euphoria at being spared a disaster with the flower harvest lasted until next morning. She slept well but her slumbers were shattered abruptly at an early hour. Zoe, looking completely distraught, came into Vicki's bedroom and shook her awake.

'I'm so sorry to have to wake you, darling. Goodness knows, you deserve your sleep. But I can't cope on my own any more.'

'What is it?' Vicki was immediately alert. 'Is it Cat?'

'No, no, she's still asleep. It's your father. He's been getting more feverish ever since he woke in the night coughing. Now his breathing is terrible and I'm so afraid . . . '

She broke off, large eyes looking desperately at Vicki. They said plainly that Zoe believed Vicki would cope.

Vicki always knew what to do for the best. So much touching faith was flattering but a heavy responsibility.

'Don't worry, Mother, I'll come right away. Have you rung the doctor?'

'Not yet. I thought I ought to wait until surgery time.'

Vicki closed her lips on a sharp retort. If Frederick was as ill as Zoe seemed to think, then of course the doctor should have been sent for — surgery time or not! Getting up hastily, she dragged on some clothes.

'Go back to him now. I'll be with you as soon as I've rung the doctor.'

'Oh, thank you.'

Zoe hurried away again, much relieved to be sharing the responsibility with capable hands.

Vicki got through to their doctor's house and tried to explain.

'He went out into the fields in that storm yesterday. I'm afraid he might have been there some time before we saw him and made him go back indoors.'

Dr Stephens was exasperated.

'Typical! The man was always as stubborn as a mule. What use could he be with a broken collarbone and a weak chest?'

'A weak chest?' Vicki repeated, puzzled.

'Didn't you know? He's had the problem for over a year. I'll be round as soon as I can.'

He put down the phone, and Vicki, too, replaced the receiver, deep in thought. So her father had a respiratory complaint! Why had he kept it from them? Memories returned of seeing him wracked by coughing. All enquiries had been met by an airy, 'Oh I've just picked up a cold.'

What a proud, foolish man he was, to think they would despise him for a physical weakness. So that was why he hadn't worked in the fields so much of late. Shaking her head in bafflement, she went to her parents' bedroom, which overlooked the fields at the back.

As soon as she got near the door she

was shocked to hear the sound of Frederick's breathing. Zoe's fears had not been exaggerated. The rasping sounds reached her 'way down the corridor.

Seeing him was even worse! Grey-faced, with the dreadful wracking, drawing of breath shaking his whole body, he was a pitiful sight. Zoe was hovering over the bed, clearly distressed.

'You see?' she whispered, looking imploringly at Vicki as though expecting her to wave a magic wand and put everything right. 'He's in such pain.'

'Mother, you should have rung the doctor earlier.'

Vicki didn't continue. What use were recriminations now? Instead she went up and sat on the bed taking hold of her father's hand rather awkwardly, remembering that that was exactly what she had done at the time of his accident. His eyes had been closed but he opened them and looked at her. She saw deep anxiety in them, anxiety that seemed to deepen as he realised who it was sitting beside him.

She said soothingly, 'Father I've rung the doctor. He'll be here shortly.'

Frederick looked unconvinced. Between the painful breaths, he managed to gasp out to Zoe, 'Leave us alone, my dear. I need to talk to Vicki — while there's still time.'

Strangely, she seemed to know what he wanted to say to her elder daughter without asking. In an agony of indecision, she looked from one to the other of them. Vicki said reasonably, 'If there's something you want to say to me, surely it doesn't matter about Mother hearing it?'

Irritation and the frustration of having his will crossed, added to the distress on Frederick's face. He began to cough, and Zoe, fearful of making him worse, got up and hurried away.

'I'll be in the kitchen, Vicki.'

She cast a frightened look at her husband and an oddly imploring one at her daughter and was gone.

Vicki waited quietly for the coughing fit to subside. After it was over, he seemed better and lay back on his pillows, spent, but still determined to have his say.

'Got to tell you, Vicki. About the will . . . only fair . . . always knew we'd have to one day.'

Vicki waited. She had absolutely no idea of what he was getting at but whatever it was, his illness was probably colouring his judgement, and it was probably no more than a storm in a teacup. She would let him talk and then, when he'd got it off his chest, he'd be able to relax.

'The farm,' he said. 'I've left it to Catriona — and Matthew. Not you.'

It took a while for the sense of what he had said to sink in. Vicki felt detached, as though the shock of what she was hearing was happening to someone else. Until now it had never occurred to her to think about what they would inherit. Had it crossed her mind at all she would simply have expected that all the property would automatically be split three ways.

When the truth penetrated, she was conscious of a feeling of unreality. Could it be true that she, who had run the whole business for years, was to be excluded from the ownership?

'But why?' The protest, the hurt, angry disbelief that he would do this, burst explosively from her lips. 'Why cut me out, Father? What have I done to deserve that?'

'Nothing.' Frederick looked conscience-stricken. 'You've done nothing. Not your fault.'

Vicki was bewildered. 'There has to be a reason. How can I accept . . . you must tell me everything.'

Frederick was lying back with his eyes closed again. Downstairs, there was the sound of voices and doors opening and closing. Vicki said urgently, 'That's probably the doctor. Father — '

Frederick seemed to make a supreme effort. Leaning forward, he said, 'You're not our daughter. We adopted you.

Thought we were never going to have our own children — didn't think we could. Then, two years later, Catriona arrived. Seemed like a miracle!'

Footsteps were coming up the stairs and Zoe's voice could be heard as she and Dr Stephens came along the upstairs corridor.

'I'm so thankful that you've come. I've never seen him like this before, and really . . . ' She broke off as the bedroom door opened and Vicki came out.

'Oh, Vicki, darling.'

She put out a hand as though to try to stop her, but Vicki, white and shaken, pushed past, not even acknowledging the presence of the doctor. Zoe gazed after her. Never before had Vicki looked like that, with all the colour drained from her face and her enormous eyes staring sightlessly ahead of her. Had Frederick told her then?

Zoe was torn with the need to be in two places at once. She knew that she ought to go after Vicki — but she couldn't leave Frederick! Her heart was wrung. In just a few weeks, their family life had become as spiked with troubles as a forest of thistles. But now she must stay with her husband. He came first, as he always had.

She clung to the belief that Frederick would be all right — she had to! If he were, everything, she was sure, could be sorted out. But, oh dear, whatever must Vicki be going through now!

★　★　★

Vicki was in her own private nightmare. She had no idea where she was heading. All she knew was that she had to get away — away from the farmhouse. Her home — which was not, after all, to be part of her future — had turned into a prison.

She walked blindly, the fresh, morning air beginning to reach her consciousness. Without slowing her pace, she took great gulps of it. So much was beginning to make sense, as her tortured thoughts took over. Catriona had always been the favourite — of course she had, she was the longed-for first child of their own, the child they had thought they would never have.

When she reached the cliff path, a new thought struck her. She stopped and said it out loud.

'Who am I? Where did I come from?'

Her words were lost in the wind. A sob rose in her throat. Without knowing it, she began to run, as though she could escape from the horrible knowledge that she did not belong to her family, that she had suddenly, in the space of half-an-hour, become a displaced person, a stranger amongst strangers.

The path was muddy from yesterday's downpour and her feet began to slide, but she didn't stop running. Around the next bend, in the lea of a windswept tree, she cannoned straight into someone.

Zak had been lining up a shot of

breakers on the beach below. As Vicki crashed into him, he grasped the distraught girl by the shoulders and prevented her from falling.

'Vicki!'

He looked down at her ravaged face and drew her back into the shelter of the tree, still holding her, arms wrapped tightly around her.

'Calm down, you're all right now.'

He didn't ask what was wrong, simply lent the comfort of his closeness and waited for her to tell him. Vicki was much too far gone to try to hide anything from him and it was all blurted out at once.

'I was adopted!' she wailed. 'My father — only he's not my father — is ill, and he's told me — I'm not even going to get a share of the farm. Oh, God, I'm nobody — I don't even know who I am.'

'You're exactly who you were before,' Zak said softly. 'A brave, hardworking, capable — and beautiful — girl. Nothing has changed. Hang on to that!'

126

'But I don't have any family.'

Vicki knew she sounded like a three-year-old. Having her whole world crash down around her ears in a matter of minutes had reduced her to feeling exactly like that — a helpless, vulnerable child. Zak was a great comfort.

He had totally accepted the situation without having to ask any more questions. And it was just what she needed, having someone praise her, and let her pour it all out. It didn't occur to her to wonder why she knew instinctively that Zak would be in her corner. All she knew was that his quiet strength let her feel she was free to be completely honest.

'All they think about is Cat,' she said bitterly. 'I've never been anything but second best.'

'Not with Cecily,' Zak said at once. 'I've talked a lot with her and she thinks you're the tops. As does anyone with eyes to see. Anyway it's not a competition, Vicki — it's life. Cat is a law unto herself! And you're someone completely different, thank goodness.'

Vicki stirred guiltily and tried to pull herself together. She had to remind herself that these arms holding her so comfortingly belonged to Catriona's friend, the one who had come with her to the island.

'I'm sorry.' She said it with contrition. 'I was just so shocked.'

'Of course you were.' Zak, looking down at her, spoke gently. 'Let me take you to your aunt's place. We can't stay here — and I think you need to be somewhere warm and have a hot drink.'

Vicki nodded. It felt right not to be in charge, for once, not to be making decisions.

'Yes, please. And thanks — for being there. I really needed someone.'

He released her but only in order to take her hand in a firm grasp and lead her away, letting it go only when they reached Cecily's cottage. One quick look at Vicki's face was all Cecily needed to know that something was badly wrong. Zak answered her questioning look briefly.

'Frederick is ill, and for some reason he has chosen now to tell Vicki that she was adopted.'

'Oh, no!' Cecily looked shattered. She crumpled on to one of the kitchen chairs. 'All this time — and he blurts it out just like that.'

'So you knew already!' Vicki was incensed. 'I suppose everyone did. I suppose I'm the only idiot who was in the dark.'

'No, that isn't true.' Cecily hurried to reassure her. 'The other two — Catriona and Matthew — they know nothing.'

'Oh.' Vicki looked a little appeased. She announced with sudden decision, 'I'm not going to stay in the dark though. I'm going to find my real parents — no matter how long it takes. I need an identity.'

Cecily's chuckle held no mirth whatsoever.

'Are you indeed? So Frederick hasn't

told you everything.'

'It feels as though my whole family has been taken away,' Vicki said, miserably. 'Even you! I'm not related to you — I'm not your real niece.'

'No, you're not my niece.' Cecily agreed, quietly.

After a moment's silence, unusual for her, she raised her eyes and met Zak's intense gaze.

'You've guessed the truth, haven't you?'

He nodded gently.

'It wasn't difficult. The dark hair among all those blondes — and I overheard a comment the other night about history repeating itself.'

Vicki looked at them both. Was this yet another conspiracy from which she was barred?

'What are you talking about?' she asked.

Cecily's face betrayed nothing of how she felt. Maintaining a calmness she was very far from feeling, she said bluntly, 'If you're going to go looking for your real parents, you won't have to go far.'

The truth dawned on Vicki like the parting of the clouds.

'You!' She gasped. 'You're my — my mother!'

'Yes.' Cecily made no move to embrace her, but she swallowed hard as her eyes scanned the girl's face anxiously. 'I'm sorry you had to find out this way. Do you mind very much?'

Zak had moved away tactfully and was filling the kettle. Now with his back towards them, Vicki sat down and took both Cecily's hands. Tears were close but neither of them let the depth of mixed emotions spill over. For the first time, they gazed into each others eyes as mother and daughter.

'I feel so confused,' Vicki said huskily. 'Disorientated! Perhaps I should have known. Cat was always the favourite — and will you tell me about it — and about my father?'

'In time!' Cecily said. 'But not right now. Just don't think too badly of us all.

It seemed the perfect answer at the time, all those years ago. Regrets came later. They desperately wanted a child and offered to take my baby. I let them — and went on a long sailing cruise after you were born. When I came back, it was too late to reclaim you.' She paused before continuing quietly.

'As for your real father, he's not a bad man. It just happened. He was much older than me — and married, with a family.'

'Did he know about me?' Vicki was almost too scared to ask the question.

'Yes. We've kept in touch. He's done what he could,' Cecily replied.

Zak put mugs of coffee in front of each of them. Vicki cupped both hands around hers, and whispered, 'You should have kept me. It would have been better to have been brought up by a single parent than become a dogs-body.'

Cecily's eyes were bright with unshed tears.

'Do you think I enjoyed watching you

work so hard and be the mainstay of the family without getting any of the glory? By then there was nothing I could do without upsetting the whole apple cart — except be here for you. That was the chief reason I moved back to the island.'

Zak sat down with them.

'It's probably none of my business but I should say you're a lot more than a dogsbody, Vicki. They all turn to you — you have status in the family.'

'Do I?' Vicki was unable to keep the note of sarcasm out of her voice.

'Yes, he's right,' Cecily said sharply. 'Don't blame Frederick for not leaving you anything. I told him long ago that you would come in for everything I have, and that's not to be sneezed at.'

'Vicki,' Zak said quietly. 'I think it's time you went home — and made your peace with . . . '

' . . . with my uncle and aunt,' Vicki finished ironically. Nonetheless she got up. 'You're right, though. I must get back to the farm. See how she is

— talk to Zoe!'

She looked at Cecily. 'I'll come back when things are less hectic. We'll have that talk.'

Cecily nodded. 'I'll look forward to it,' she said quietly and opened the door for her to go out.

Zak put his arm round the older woman's shoulders as they watched Vicki head off towards the place she'd called home for so many years.

7

It was difficult, as Vicki had known it would be, returning to the farm and facing Zoe. She found her in her studio, absorbed in painting a watercolour. That was predictable! In times of trouble, painting had always been Zoe's solace.

When she saw Vicki, she put down her brushes and came towards her, arms outstretched.

'Oh, Vicki, my dear, I've been so worried. Where have you been? The doctor gave Fred an injection and he's asleep. His breathing is better already. I would have come looking for you if I'd only known which way you'd gone.'

Vicki was enveloped in a hug. Her heart twisted. Zoe always smelt of flower fragrances, and the closeness reminded her of the times in childhood when her mother had hugged her and kissed away her tears. But her mother, as she'd known her, was not her mother!

'I went to see Cecily,' she said and saw an immediate reaction in Zoe's eyes.

In answer to the unspoken, apprehensive question, Vicki spoke quietly.

'Yes, I know now that Cecily is my birth mother. Why did you all act a lie? Why wasn't I told the truth years ago? It might not have been such a shock learning it then as it was today, when Father thought he was on his death bed.'

'Don't. Please, don't say that.' Zoe couldn't bear even to hear the word death in connection with her beloved husband. 'He's going to be all right,' she asserted quickly. 'Doctor Stephens assured me it would only take a week or so of rest and medication to restore him. But we have to take a lot more care of him from now on.'

She was silent a moment, twisting her hands agitatedly in and out of the paint rags she still held.

'Can you forgive us? About bringing you up as our own child? We only did what we thought was best for you — for everyone — at the time.'

There was a footstep behind them and they both turned. Catriona was standing there, looking, for once, completely serious. Vicki, with unconscious irony, addressed her as she usually did.

'Hello, sis.'

Catriona came swiftly across the room to her. It was obvious from the sympathetic look on her face that she had been told. Probably, Vicki thought, Zoe had needed to share her worries with someone, while she herself had been missing.

'I'm glad you're still saying that. You'll always be my sister,' Catriona affirmed. 'It's just a storm in a tea-cup, doesn't make any difference to me — and it won't to Matt when he comes home and finds out.'

She sounded as though she were

talking about a grazed knee. One just needs to put on a plaster and all will be well! Vicki recognised that Catriona meant to be kind but she had no conception of the devastating shock of finding out, at twenty-eight, that you were adopted — not the person you thought you were.

Vicki spoke evenly. 'It does make a difference but thanks anyway. I need to think and get used to the idea. Right now, I'm going over to see Steve. After that, I'll be joining the girls in the fields, but we'll be together tonight. Can you cope with dinner?'

'Yes, of course' they chorused before smiling at each other.

There was a general feeling of relief emanating from them. Perhaps they had expected her to create a scene — to throw a tantrum, though they should have known that was not her style. Her immediate emotional outburst had been shared with Zak on the clifftop. After that she had reverted to her usual personality.

The other two, glad that the first encounter was over without a dreadful scene, immediately set to work planning the evening's menu. As Vicki left the room, they were already arguing about the merits of lamb or chicken.

From the doorway, she cast a quick look back. Two blonde heads, she thought, peas in a pod. In a few years' time, Cat would be just like Zoe. She shivered as she opened the kitchen door and felt the chilly air outside. It was symbolic! No wonder she had always felt out in the cold in this family — she really wasn't one of them at all.

The walk to the stables gave her time to look forward to seeing Steve. Her spirits began to rise. The others had been her past, he was her present and her future. And of course, he, of them all, would surely understand the enormity of what she had learned today. It would be so good to have him reassure her, to be there for her, an ally, a supporter. The anticipation was heartwarming, and she began to hurry.

Steve was in his house, dealing with a desk full of papers, his small computer turned on. He got up quickly when she came in.

'Vicki, are you all right?'

'No, not really.' She went unselfconsciously forward, putting her arms about him and laying her head against his shoulder. 'Oh, Steve, I've had such a ghastly day.'

'I know.' He patted her back awkwardly.

'You know?' Vicki turned her head and looked up at him in surprise. He said, with a touch of constraint, 'They rang me — and told me. It's unbelievable.'

Vicki stepped back. 'I see.' She was conscious of a quickly-suppressed sense of grievance. Surely it was her prerogative to break such momentous news concerning herself — at least to Steve!

She looked around. The papers on his desk were neatly arranged in piles. Had he really been able to concentrate on all this, after knowing that she was in

140

such trouble? She wondered forlornly why he had not come looking for her. Couldn't he have guessed what torment she must be in?

Steve continued. 'Poor Catriona was in quite a state, almost incoherent, in fact. We — both of us — found it incredible that they'd kept such a secret all this time. It must have been the most awful shock for you, Vicki.'

'Yes, it was.'

Vicki's sense of disappointment grew. If he was able to appreciate that the news had shaken Catriona, what did he think it had done to her? A sense of unreality was creeping over her. There was something unpleasant hovering at the back of her mind. Was it fear — or a stomach-churning knowledge she was not yet capable of facing? Was this Steve, the one who was going to be with her in sickness and in health?

What she felt now was a kind of sickness — and he certainly wasn't sharing it. He was mouthing the right things but there was none of the warmth, the feeling, or the understanding that she had hoped for — or that she had a right to expect.

He seemed distant, distracted, even uncertain how to treat her. A dreadful suspicion entered her head. Could Steve have heard that she was no longer going to inherit the farm? Had that altered his attitude towards her? She hated mistrusting him but had to test her theory.

'My father — I mean, Frederick, has told me he's not left me anything.'

She waited tensely for his reaction, deliberately saying nothing about inheriting from Cecily. Steve's eyes opened wide in amazement.

'What? After the way you've kept them going — and all the work you've put in on the farm? That's the most unjust thing I've ever heard!'

He sounded genuinely horrified and Vicki, relieved, absconded him, at least from having had prior knowledge of that. It had been a base suspicion and she was ashamed of herself.

Yet still they stood, a foot apart, like uneasy strangers. Unbidden, the memory returned of the instant empathy she had had from Zak, the newcomer. Steve was her long-time friend — the man she was going to marry. She felt desperately let down. It was as though he were in a glass case that kept him from her. She was intinctively sure that whatever she said, whatever she did, he would remain withdrawn and apart.

The small window above Steve's desk blew open, with a noisy clatter. He went to fix the catch with an air of relief, as though glad to have something definite to do. With his back half-turned, still reaching up, he said off-handedly, 'Vicki, I'm sorry but I'm really pushed for time right now. I'll come down to the farm tonight, if that's all right. I'll hear all about it then. Is that OK?'

So she was being dismissed! Far from wanting to be alone with her, he was suggesting a meeting in the midst of the family circle. Vicki felt as though she had been slapped in the face. She licked dry lips and mustered up a small, tight smile, determined to retain her pride. If that was the way he wanted it, right! She would not even acknowledge that she knew something was wrong. She would wait until he was ready to tell her.

Her casual tone, when she replied, matched his.

'Of course it's all right. I'll see you tonight.'

Somehow she lifted her hand in a would-be cheery wave. Somehow she got out of the door. Somehow she walked away. And no watcher would have known, from the erectness of her back, that a nightmare was engulfing her.

★　★　★

Several hours with the other girls, picking and packing daffodils like an automaton, was therapeutic and did much to restore normality.

Nothing could still the racing adrenalin in her body or the whirling of her brain but at least her thoughts managed to convince her that the strangeness of the scene with Steve had been a figment of her imagination. She had to be wrong! Her perception of the whole scene had been faulty, that must be it!

The events of today had been so traumatic that she had simply expected too much. Everyone knew that men found it difficult to express sympathy or emotion. Tonight he would be his old self again. And she would be able to laugh at her fears!

Back at the farmhouse, her nose registered a fragrant aroma of roasting lamb and rosemary. Zoe had wanted chicken so, predictably, Catriona had won the argument! Well, that was the way it was — Catriona was one of life's winners.

But for now, it would be good to be served a meal she had not had to cook or organise for herself. First a visit to try and put Frederick's mind at rest — she dreaded that but it had to be done — and then a long, hot bath.

When she tapped on the door and tiptoed into his bedroom, Frederick was asleep, his breathing, mercifully, much quieter. Glad to be able to postpone the difficult meeting, she did not disturb him but went instead to the bathroom and ran the water in the big, old-fashioned bath.

She took her time for once, and let her tired muscles relax in the hot bubbles. By the time she came down to dinner she felt better and less tense than she had since the rude awakening of the early morning.

Efforts had certainly been made to create a pleasant atmosphere in the dining-room. Lamps were lit and there was a log fire in the old grate. The table was laid with the best linen and decorated with crystal and flowers. Zoe appeared with a tray of sherry.

'Well, dear, what do you think? It's nearly all Catriona's doing. She's worked so hard, even made a lemon mousse. Fred is asleep but I'll take him something later. We were so anxious to have a nice meal for you, to show you how much you mean to us. Dinner is nearly ready to serve, but I said we must have a little drink together first — just the three of us.'

'That would be lovely.'

Vicki's lips twitched. They were being so thoughtful and so careful to put her first. For the only time in her life she was being treated like the prodigal daughter. And it was all to hide the fact that today was the day she had learned she was not the daughter at all. Life, so it seemed, was full of surprises. It was a switchback. Now you go down, now you go up!

Catriona was not far behind her mother. She was looking quite unlike her usual immaculate self, with a big apron over her dress and flushed cheeks from the heat of cooking.

She sipped her sherry, saying chattily, 'I suppose, in my condition, I should stay off this but I feel so much better now the first three months are over.'

She looked sunnily around at the other two, seemingly perfectly ready to believe that all the unpleasantness was over and everything was completely back to normal.

'Isn't this nice — all the Jamieson females together?'

Vicki realised she hadn't considered what her surname would be.

'Yes, you're right. I am still called Jamieson.'

'I should think so.' Zoe sounded quite annoyed. 'We're all the same blood family.' A trace of anxiety clouded her brow. 'I hope it's not going to be too difficult explaining to Matthew when he comes home at the week-end. Was Steve very shocked when you told him?'

Vicki, surprised, said, 'But Steve already knew. I thought you'd rung him.'

'No, that was me, actually.' Catriona said it casually but her cheeks were again carrying a rosy glow. 'Perhaps I should have waited until you told him yourself.'

'It doesn't matter. But he's coming over tonight. If he arrives before we've finished eating ... ' Vicki didn't manage to finish her sentence.

'Oh, there'll be plenty. It won't take a moment to lay an extra place. I've cooked a huge joint and masses of lovely vegetables.' Catriona was clearly proud of her efforts. 'Sit down, Vicki. You're not to do a thing except be waited on. Mother, come and help me bring it in.'

They both left the room, but were back again within minutes, this time pushing the hot trolley and accompanied by Steve.

'He came in through the kitchen,' Catriona explained gaily. She looked roguishly up at him. 'You'll be able to see what a wonderful cook I can be when I try.'

Just like Zoe, Vicki thought. She can rise to any occasion.

Steve had not yet glanced in his

fiancée's direction. Now he did and said, with a trace of formality, 'You look nice.'

Vicki's spirits had plummeted again. No, she had not imagined it — he was the same man she had met this afternoon. The horrible glass case was still there between them! He was just making a public effort. After only a momentary hesitation, he came forward, leaned down and kissed her on the cheek.

Zoe smiled at them indulgently, quite unaware of any tension. She sighed happily. 'Now we can all have a relaxed, family dinner.'

Obediently, they took their places at the table but, in fact, Zoe was the only one to enjoy a relaxed, family dinner. The others were all in their own private versions of torture, Vicki from a growing certainty that her love was her love no longer.

Matters came to a head later in the evening, after Vicki had gone upstairs with Zoe to see her father. Once he was awake, Zoe had taken him a tray and reported joyously that he had been well enough to eat it and would like to see Vicki. So there was no help for it!

In the event, the interview was not as bad as she had anticipated. The Frederick she found tonight was neither the autocratic father she was used to nor the sick and remorseful man he had been earlier in the day. True, he was still chastened and it was strange to be asked for her forgiveness but she had no hesitation in giving it.

They talked a while and he asked her if she were still willing to run the business.

'I don't know.' Vicki was honest. 'I'll certainly see this harvest in. It's nearly finished anyway. But after that, I truly don't know.'

'You must be free to do whatever you want. But since you'll only be living up the road . . . ' Zoe began.

'Give me time. I want to find out who my real father is and — other

151

things,' Vicki pleaded, and could suddenly stand it no longer.

The pained expression that had flickered across Frederick's face, the reproachful one on Zoe's. It was all too much! There had been too many emotional happenings today. It was too soon to be talking about making plans and they must accept that. Abruptly she got up from her chair.

'I'll go downstairs now. No, don't you leave him,' she added as Zoe rose, too. 'You stay and talk. I'll be all right.'

She carried the memory of their worried faces with her as she reached the head of the stairs. The upstairs carpet was thick and her footsteps made no sound as she began to descend. Voices, slightly muffled, but still easy to hear, were coming from behind the dining-room door which was not quite closed.

'Darling, we can't possibly tell Vicki now. If you thought you were coming here tonight so as to break it to her, it's just not on. She's had quite enough to bear today without that.'

'I know — but what are we to do? She has to know sometime. We ought not to wait too long to get married — because of the baby.'

There was a momentary silence which the still figure on the stairs had no trouble interpreting. Catriona and Steve were kissing! Then came Catriona's voice, warm and loving.

'You're the most wonderful person in the world. It's so good of you — so kind, you know, to accept another man's child.'

Steve's answer, delivered in a low voice, killed for ever the last of Vicki's illusions.

'It's not good, or kind of me. It's because, my gorgeous girl, I've always loved you — and I always will.'

Vicki wondered, almost with a sense of detachment, how much more she could take. In one day she had lost everyone — mother, father, sister, brother, and now her husband-to-be. Most of them had been deceiving her.

All of them, intentionally or not, had been living a lie. She tore frantically at the diamond ring on her finger and had succeeded in tugging it off by the time she pushed open the dining-room door. The two inside sprang apart hurriedly.

She extended her hand towards Steve, palm upwards with the ring on it.

'Yours, I think.' Her voice was as brittle as the diamond she held.

'Oh, Vicki, I'm sorry. We didn't want to hurt you.' Catriona looked aghast.

'Didn't you? Then I'll try not to mind too much.' Vicki gave an apology of a smile, her eyes on Steve. 'It doesn't seem to be my day, does it? Just do me a favour, Catriona — please don't ask me to be a bridesmaid.'

She had to get away before she broke down. Neither of them was going to see her cry, whatever happened. Before she left the room, she managed to turn for one last comment.

'I hope you'll both be very happy,' she said, 'because I honestly believe you deserve each other.'

8

The next day had a washed, clean air about it. Early spring days on the island were often like that. When Vicki walked across the beach, she saw guillemots swooping and resting on the edge of foam-crested waves. They looked carefree and at one with the elements.

She wished she were one of them. She wished passionately that she could escape from herself, and from the sense of living in an unreal world, peopled by strangers, that the events of the last twenty-four hours had left her. It was tempting to take out a dinghy for an hour but one look at the water had persuaded her it was much too wild. Not that she was scared, but no-one should have the chance to wonder if she had decided to end it all!

If yesterday had signalled a personal holocaust, a night of tossing and turning had solved nothing — except to harden the resolve that she must start again. But where? And how? For the first time she bitterly regretted that she had been the stay-at-home daughter, who had acquired no qualifications or training, other than being able to run a house and a flower farm.

She discounted her abilities, knowledge and managerial skills. In her present mood, everything appeared completely negative and she felt that she had never really done anything or been anywhere on her own.

'I'm an inadequate,' she said out loud, feet scuffing the sand, and hands driven deep into her jacket pockets. 'I've been cocooned in the nest all my life and now I've got to fly. And I will. If only I knew in which direction!'

With sudden relief she remembered another nest, where she was sure there would always be a place for her, not to hide, but to shelter and use as a temporary refuge. Turning sharply, she went back across the beach towards

Cecily's cottage.

As she neared the path across the dunes, she could see the cottage in the distance and it was clear Cecily had visitors. The island taxi had drawn up outside and the driver was helping someone out. The man, an elderly gentleman, was vaguely familiar and Vicki recalled seeing him about the island a few times recently.

How long would he be staying, she wondered, as she impatiently wheeled about and retraced her footsteps. Until that moment of huge disappointment, she hadn't realised how anxious she was to see Cecily and have the talk they had promised each other.

The tide had turned. As Vicki walked between two twenty-foot-high slabs of grey rock she saw that the waves were no longer reaching the line of seaweed and debris halfway up the beach. She was making for the long, stone breakwater, to walk out on it, when she saw a column of smoke rising in the air. A distant figure was feeding a bonfire he had lit at the back of the beach. Zak!

Vicki hesitated. Zak had been so good yesterday — but he knew nothing as yet about the break-up of her engagement. She had been enough of a burden to him. Apart from which, she thought grimly, she wasn't certain how he would feel about Catriona getting married. No, she would avoid him today — let him enjoy whatever he had come to do.

She would not inflict her own troubles on him. Besides, the last thing she wanted was for him, or anyone else, to feel sorry for her. For the second time in half an hour, Vicki turned and headed in the opposite direction.

★ ★ ★

Zak had made the bonfire on impulse. He was intent on photographing the friendly puffins, but standing around was a chilly business. There was so much driftwood lying about he had decided to make himself a fire to return to when he wanted to warm up.

Staying away from Vicki and the farm had been a conscious decision, but he had discussed it with Cecily who was happy to air her view.

'I'm letting them alone,' she had announced firmly. 'If she needs me she knows where to find me.'

And me, Zak thought, hoping Vicki did indeed know that he was available in whatever rôle she needed.

He had applauded Cecily's resolute stance. Not making any claim on her daughter, letting her adoptive family have their say, without influence from her, was a brave act in his eyes and he told her so. For a vulnerable moment, the naked longing she worked so hard to hide showed on Cecily's face. Then she had quickly reverted to her normal self, saying gruffly, 'And I want you out of the house for an hour or so this morning, Zak, my lad. Got a visitor.'

'Assignations eh?' he teased. 'But don't worry. I've got an assignation,

too, hopefully with gulls, terns, razor-
bills and puffins!'

* * *

Intent on his cameras and the building
of his fire, Zak did not see Vicki when
she first spotted him, nor when she
turned and headed in the other
direction. He was enjoying watching
sparks fizzle off the dried-out wood.
Watching a fire burn was, he decided
contentedly, second only to watching
the constant movement of water, and
here he was doing both! A beach-
comber — with times to stand and
stare!

What a wonderful change it all was
from the pressures of living in London,
taking the photographs he wanted to
take instead of those he was assigned,
that were commercially viable. If his
career continued on the path of
success, he would buy a holiday home
here on the island.

His train of thought was broken

when he heard a distant cry and was suddenly alert. A flock of gulls was screeching loudly overhead. He must have been mistaken in taking it for a human voice, he decided. Something had disturbed them though, he mused.

They had all risen screamingly into the air, on the other side of the breakwater. Zak wondered if it could be a seal. If so, he would like to catch it on film. He hurried to the breakwater and clambered up the slippery stone sides. From the top he could see right across the width of the beach and what he saw startled him into an involuntary shout of horror. A woman was struggling in the water!

Zak flung down his camera and began to run. If he could get to the edge of the rocks nearest her, he might be able to reach her. There was no-one else around — a cursory glance had already shown him that. He was her only hope.

He could see, as he got close, that she was swimming strongly, but the waves and the current had already swept her farther away from the rocks. She might stay afloat, but getting back to land would be a different matter.

He was already on the low rocks before he realised, with a sickening lurch of fear, who the woman was!

'Vicki! Hold on — I'm coming!'

She could see him but he didn't know if she could hear him. No, she was too far from the rocks for him to reach. With a fatalistic certainty that he would be no better in the water than she, he had still begun frantically tugging at his jacket when he saw a tree branch lying on the beach. It looked long enough to make up the distance between Vicki and the rocks. If only she wasn't swept farther out while he fetched it . . .

Fear lent wings to his feet and strength to his arms. Within seconds he had sprinted over to where it was lying and dragged it back. He was filled with a desperate longing to let her know he was not afraid to go in after her and was not deserting her. But commonsense told him that he had a much better chance of saving her this way.

Vicki saw what he was doing, and redoubled her efforts not to be swept farther away. When she had slipped off the rocks, despair and helplessness had enveloped her but that had gone as soon as she saw Zak. If he failed in his attempt, she knew he would alert someone, get the lifeboat out, rescue her somehow. As long as she could keep swimming!

Breathing hard, Zak forced the big branch out across the water, praying that it was long enough. He dug his feet into the edge of a rock. If he were pulled in, so be it. He had meant to go in for her anyway, and would be no worse off!

He held the branch and waited. The next surge of a wave, the next strokes she made, she would be there. His heart seemed to stop beating as his foot almost slipped — he was bent back so low, he was virtually on the ground.

Vicki was tiring but she knew it was now or never. The branch was tantalisingly close. But the top of it was light — what if it snapped and broke off when she grasped it? No use thinking of that. She reached for it and felt the twigs in her palms. The water tried to pull her away but she reached again — and again — and again. Each time she was getting farther up the branch. Her hold was stronger now and Zak, sure that she had a good hold, was dragging it in. Slowly, slowly, she was against the rocks, on the rocks, and had grasped his hands, was in his arms. She fell against him, sobbing with relief and exhaustion.

Dimly she was aware that he was angry, that he was muttering something over her head.

'You stupid, crazy, little fool. What did you think you were doing?'

She was shaking with sudden chills but still had the spirit to snap back.

'Are you saying I did it on purpose? Of course I didn't. I slipped, you idiot.'

She had sat up and pulled away from him and her wet face, the hair plastered to her head, looked furious. Zak's own face softened as he looked at her. Without any intention of doing so, he pulled her back towards him and kissed her hard on the mouth. It was a statement, an exultant assertion of thankfulness that she was still alive and safe!

When he drew away he said shakily, 'Don't be such a heroine or I'll throw you back into the sea.'

Vicki, who was deeply affected by the passion behind the kiss, was beginning to tremble from both reaction and cold. She said remorsefully, 'You saved my life, and I didn't even say thank you.'

Zak, who was gathering her up and clutching her to him as though she weren't completely sodden, said tersely, 'Never mind all that. We've got to get you back to the farm and dry you out. What am I thinking about, wasting time like this?'

'No!' Vicki almost shouted it. 'I don't

want to go home — or to the cottage. I won't. You can't make me. Please! Just let me dry out by your fire.'

Zak thought fast. He was unhappy at letting her stay outdoors, but she was obviously distraught. Perhaps he had better humour her.

'All right. Come on, then. But you've got to get out of those wet things.'

He took her hand and led her back across the breakwater to his still blazing fire, setting a fast pace so that she was running. When they reached it, Vicki sank down beside the blaze.

'No, you don't.' Zak pulled her up again. 'Get out of those wet things. And put this blanket round you. Thank goodness I was planning to stay out for the day and had my backpack with me. Don't worry — I won't look.'

While she was stripping off, he went back to the wall and picked up his cameras. Then he returned, took a towel and his flask out of his backpack and poured her a mug of coffee. By then, she was wrapped in the old blanket Cecily had lent him to sit on. Silently he handed her the mug but her teeth were chattering when she tried to drink it.

Acting by instinct, Zak sat down beside her and wrapped her in his arms, his only conscious motive a desire to lend her the warmth of his own body. Vicki smiled gratefully at him and sipped from the mug. After a little while, the shivering stopped.

When she handed the empty mug back to him, he put it on the sand and began to towel her wet hair. There was a curious intimacy about the homely act. After a moment Vicki protested.

'Ouch, don't be so rough. Anyway the fire is drying it out. I'm steaming.'

She laughed, and Zak dropped the towel. Her smiling face was only a few inches from his own.

Their eyes locked, his expression serious, his brows drawn together in a questioning look. Vicki saw that he wanted to kiss her again but would not if she refused. A flood of feeling, a depth of emotion she had never known for anyone before, swept over her. Without even thinking about it, she withdrew her arms from the blanket and put them around his neck. Zak's lips met hers in a gesture of love, passion and tenderness that filled them both with longing.

'Vicki, I'm sorry, but I love you.'

They had stopped to draw breath and he said it in a sort of groan, their mouths still nearly touching.

Vicki murmured, 'Why sorry? Oh, I know — Steve. We broke up last night. He's going to marry Catriona.'

'My darling!' Zak sat back, and held her at arms length. He said tenderly, 'That really must have been the last straw. Are you sure you weren't trying to end it all yourself?'

Vicki pulled the blanket tighter around her. She injected as much coldness into her voice as she could. 'You've just said you love me — and yet you think I would do that. How could you?'

'No, of course not.' He was apologetic. 'But you must have been feeling dreadful — after all that happened yesterday — then this. Tell me about it.'

She told him, leaning back against the dunes with his arm comfortingly warm and tight about her, and the heat of the fire warming them both through.

'So you see,' she finished up, 'Steve loved her all along.'

'Then he shouldn't have planned to marry you,' Zak said, anger in his voice. 'That was folly! They're not bad people in my view, just lightweights, who don't think things through. Anyway, never mind them. What about us?'

Vicki was too honest to be coquettish. 'I think I've fallen in love with you, too,' she said. 'You're such a tower of strength — so good — so dependable. Can you believe that? It seems incredible, right after I was going to marry someone else. But it's quite different. Truly! Until you kissed me, I didn't know how it could be. I thought that what I felt for Steve was enough.'

Zak smiled at her. 'That's wonderful. And very flattering.' He looked serious. 'I think that admiration and respect are very necessary. But there's a lot more to a relationship than that. You haven't said anything about desire.'

For an unguarded moment, his eyes dropped to where the blanket revealed creamy shoulders. 'I want you in every way,' he said. 'As a wife, as a friend, as a woman. No half-measures.'

Vicki drew a breath of sheer happiness. An hour ago, she had been in the depths of despair. Now everything had changed. But she was afraid to trust her instincts yet. She remembered the sense of failure she had had walking the beach earlier, wondering what she had achieved in life.

She said softly, 'I want you, too. But there are lots of things to settle first. I've got to be me — to find who I am, and the place to start finding out is at Cecily's.'

9

The taxi had gone from the front of Cecily's cottage, so they were reasonably sure of finding her alone. She was in the kitchen gazing thoughtfully out of the window. The front door being, as usual, unlocked, Zak didn't even have to use his key and they burst unceremoniously in on her.

When Cecily first turned and stared at them, there was a faraway look in her eyes but that rapidly changed to one of astonishment as she took in the sight before her of Vicki, sandy, salty, wrapped only in a blanket, and with her chestnut hair in wild disarray.

'Good grief! What's been happening?' She gave them no time to reply. 'Never mind, tell me later. Go straight upstairs, my girl, and get in the shower before you catch your death of cold. You stay here and heat up some soup,' she ordered Zak.

Cecily followed Vicki up the narrow stairs. Both of them had been apprehensive about the awkwardness of this first meeting, after the momentous disclosures of the last one, but the unusual circumstances prevented them feeling embarrassed.

Vicki was profoundly thankful that there was no need to agonise about how they were going to treat each other. Cecily, bossy, fond, straightforward, was exactly the way she had always been. Now she took complete charge, putting out big fluffy towels and shampoo, and running the shower. Then, while the hot water gushed over the girl like a healing balm, she herself disappeared into her bedroom.

'Laid out some clothes,' she called through the plastic curtain. 'Put them on when you're finished. Hair-dryer's on the bed. Come down when you're ready. I'll go downstairs now.'

Twenty minutes later, an infinitely refreshed Vicki joined the others in the kitchen, her hair a shining halo of brilliance. She was wearing a pair of jeans that were too big and not long enough for her and one of the men's shirts that Cecily habitually appeared in! But even in the odd assortment of garments, Zak thought that he had never seen her look more beautiful.

He wondered if it could be the shine in her eyes — unaware that his own were shining in the same way! There was a brand new aura, a glorious glow about her. He hoped, fervently, that he had been partly responsible for putting it there!

Cecily, a woman of few words, informed Vicki matter-of-factly that Zak had told her everything. Nothing Catriona did could surprise her, but she was shocked to find Steve so stupid he couldn't tell gold from dross.

Vicki, amused, gurgled delightedly. 'It's wonderful being with you two. You're totally prejudiced and — thank goodness — entirely on my side.'

Cecily glanced at her sharply. 'You

don't look too cut up about it all.'

Vicki, for one irresistible moment, met Zak's eyes and quickly looked away again.

'No, I'm not really. So you don't need to worry about me.'

'I wasn't worried.' Cecily, who had been intensely worried, hastily repudiated the ridiculous notion that she could be anxious about Vicki's well-being. 'Why should I be worried? I know you. Got too much commonsense to go overboard.'

'Hooray, somebody recognises that at last.' Vicki was triumphant. 'Zak thought I'd thrown myself in the sea on purpose — literally gone overboard. But I think I managed to convince him that wasn't true.'

Again their eyes met, his warmly ardent. This time, Cecily who was no fool, intercepted the look.

'Something between you two, is there?' she asked bluntly, and Vicki started guiltily.

'Well, yes, there is, but it's too soon. I

feel terrible, falling out of one man's arms and into another's. How could I do that? Whatever would people say?'

'Tell them to mind their own business,' Cecily offered robustly. Clearly she had no doubts on that score at all.

'Don't mind telling you I'm delighted. Had my doubts about you and Steve. I wanted you to be happy but I was afraid you wouldn't suit. Nice enough chap, hardworking — but no depth. I've got to know this fellow, here, pretty well lately. Can't sail with someone and not find out what sort of person they are. Don't mind telling you now he's worth a hundred Steves.' She patted Zak on the arm, and he grinned down at her.

'Yes, I know,' Vicki said. 'But there are some other things I have to sort out, too. I haven't had time to get used to — to not being who I thought I was. Or who I am — or even who I want to be.'

Cecily grew serious immediately. 'Drink your soup,' she said. 'There's something I was going to tell you anyway. Now seems as good a time as any.'

They sat at the table and waited, but she seemed in no hurry to begin. She was, in fact, clearly experiencing difficulty in knowing where to start.

'I suppose you want to find out who your father was?' she said eventually.

Vicki nodded vigorously, and Cecily sighed. 'Would you like to meet him?'

This time Vicki found it more difficult. Did she want to meet him?

'I'd like to know what the story is first,' she said thoughtfully. 'Did he let you down?'

'No, he didn't.' Cecily was emphatic on that point. 'I knew he was a married man with a family. He was a lot older than me, as I told you. I went into it with my eyes open. But afterwards — well, he was afraid of spoiling his family life. I didn't blame him. He has two sons and he's devoted to them. So we cut loose completely. I'd made plenty of money and I didn't need support. But he always kept in touch. Lately, though — things have changed.'

She seemed lost in a reverie of nostalgia and neither Vicki nor Zak wanted to press her. After a moment she began again and what she said sent a bolt of shock through Vicki.

'He's ill — it's terminal. He's got about six months to live — if that. He didn't want to go without seeing you. He's been here quite a while, on the island. He told his family he had to get away on his own for a bit, but he's going back tomorrow.'

'Oh, no.' Vicki was filled with rage and frustration. 'You mean I find my real father only to lose him again?'

Zak put his arm about her shoulder and Cecily looked at them coolly.

'Are you only sorry for yourself?' she enquired. 'What about him? You still have your life in front of you.'

Vicki could not recall Cecily speaking to her so severely, but the rebuke was justified. It was true that she had been thinking only of herself.

'I don't know him,' she said miserably. 'It wasn't my fault that I've never had the chance to know him. So it's hard for me to feel sorry for him — or care about him. Surely that's natural enough?'

Cecily continued. 'He asked if you would meet him, here, at four o'clock. He's going back on the five-thirty ferry. But I didn't promise. I said it would be your choice.'

'Oh!' Vicki gasped in surprise. 'Then he was the man in the taxi — the one I've seen about the farm.'

'He wanted to see you, that's all. He never thought he'd ever get a chance to meet you, face to face. But after you found out the truth, we thought it might be possible, after all. Is it?'

Vicki considered. Then she said, with decision, 'It has to be. If I refused I'd never be able to forget — or forgive myself.'

Zak intervened. 'Speaking of which, if you want to wipe the slate clean, I think you have to go back to your old family and put things right there, too. For your own sakes.'

Vicki looked at the two concerned faces and was suddenly filled with a sense of happiness. She was so lucky. Last night — or the day before — she would never have believed the next day could bring so much change. Here in this kitchen was her new family. Some deep-seated sense of certainty, part instinct, part intuition, told her that she and Zak had begun something today which would bind them together for life. As for Cecily, she had always known that she would be there for her. Now she was doubly sure.

'You're right,' she said gratefully. 'I'll go back to the farm right away.'

'But you have to mean what you say! It's got to be genuine.' Zak gave her a questioning look.

She smiled, and said teasingly, 'Are you planning to be my conscience? Yes, I'll mean it. Why not? Frederick and Zoe acted with the best of intentions. Steve and Catriona let me down, but I

honestly think they re-discovered something in each other they probably
should have recognised years ago. In
that case, it could never had worked
between me and Steve.'

'Good girl.' Cecily took her hand and
patted it. Then, as if ashamed of
showing so much feeling, she said, 'You
look pretty awful in that get-up. It'll be
just as well to get into something that
fits you before you come back and meet
Harold.'

★ ★ ★

Zoe and Catriona were both in the
farm kitchen when she reached there.
They were busy preparing dinner and
Vicki remembered with a touch of
guilty amusement that she had abandoned all her customary duties. Both
women looked up when she came in.
There was an air of uncertainty and
momentary silence as they waited to see
what she would say.

'Well, don't look at me as though I'm

a ghost. I only went for a walk to clear my head,' Vicki said lightly.

'Those clothes — they're not yours,' Zoe said.

'No, I slipped and fell in the water. Zak rescued me — Cecily lent me some things.'

'You fell in?'

Zoe's eyes were like saucers. It was quite clear what her question implied and Catriona, still seated, gave a low moan and put both hands in front of her face. It was only when she heard Vicki laugh that she took them away and looked wonderingly at her.

'Not you as well! Why does everyone think I'm the sort to hurl myself into the sea on purpose?'

She sat down and pulled Zoe gently down, too, so that they were sitting around the table facing each other.

'I'm sorry I went to bed last night without speaking to anyone and left this morning so early. But now I think it's time for a little conference.'

She turned first to Zoe. 'Do you want

me to go on calling you Mother?'

Zoe's eyes welled with tears. She nodded wordlessly.

'Then I will. Cecily wouldn't want it any other way. Things will never be the same again — and perhaps that's a good thing — but at least we're still family. In a way I've always felt more of a niece than a daughter here.'

'Oh no!' That had hit home to both of them in a way Vicki had never intended.

Zoe pleaded, 'Darling, that can't be true,' and Catriona exclaimed, 'You're my only sister — whatever the facts!'

'Am I? What you did to me wasn't very sisterly.' Vicki said it from the heart, unable to suppress what she felt was the truth.

Catriona was near to tears. She looked wretched. 'I know. You've got every right to hate me — and Steve. Do you? Please say you don't.'

'I don't. I truly don't.'

It was tempting to say that she believed they had done her the greatest service of her life but she resisted. What had happened between her and Zak must remain their secret for the moment, theirs and Cecily's.

'I understand about you and Steve but I wish he'd never got engaged to me. And I'll tell him that when I see him. Once that's over we can be friends again, and I promise you I'll dance quite happily at your wedding.'

A deep voice from the door said grimly. 'There'll be no dancing. It will be as quiet an affair as we can contrive.'

This disapproval had clearly been the theme of the day! Vicki understood suddenly why Catriona had been looking so drawn. It must have been the first time in her life she was unable to wind her father around her little finger!

Zoe got quickly up. 'Oh, Fred, you know you shouldn't be downstairs yet.'

He walked to the table and sat down heavily in one of the chairs.

'I wanted to see if Vicki was back.

And I heard what you said, my poor girl. How could they do such an underhand thing to you? It's beyond my comprehension.'

Catriona's threatened tears had become real, but for once, her father was oblivious. His sympathy was all for Vicki. She was conscious of a strong desire to relieve his mind by telling him about her own happiness but knew she could not. That must wait!

The only way she could put their minds at rest was by proving that she was not the distraught girl they had expected her to be. She did this so ably, in the next half-hour, that by the time she went upstairs to change, the atmosphere in the kitchen had lightened considerably. And they all understood each other much better!

Frederick had confided to Zoe earlier, that although he would never be anything other than a devoted father, he had shown a great lack of fairness in his treatment of his children. About Catriona, it had wrung Zoe's heart to hear him say sadly, 'I fear I am probably to blame for her instability of character, which is what has landed her in her situation. We must stand by her, no matter what.'

10

Walking back to the cottage, Vicki was possessed of a curiously unreal feeling. Could it be true that she was on her way to meet the man who was her real father? She still had a sense of disbelief about it all. Perhaps in a moment she would wake up in her bed at the farm! It would be time to get up and pick daffodils and discover the whole thing had been a dream.

Her nerves were beginning to jangle and she had butterflies in her stomach by the time she reached the door. Cecily came out to meet her, eyes anxiously scanning Vicki's face.

'You all right? Did you see Frederick?'

'Yes and everything is fine. We've all made our peace and everything is going to jog along normally from now on.'

Cecily snorted sceptically. 'Depends

what you mean by normal. If you think I'm standing by from now on and watching you turn back into a dogsbody, you can forget it.'

'No, not that. But at least we all understand each other a little better and accept what's happened.'

She was impatient to begin what she had come to do and could contain herself no longer. 'Is he here?'

Cecily nodded. 'In the sitting-room. I thought it would be best if you see him alone. I'll be in the kitchen if you need me.'

'And Zak?' It was somehow enormously important to know that Zak was near.

'In with me. He's insisted on standing by.' Cecily hesitated, then gave her an unplanned convulsive hug. 'Chin up m'dear.' It showed the amount of feeling she was too inarticulate to express. Then with a muttered, 'Don't judge him harshly,' she was gone.

★ ★ ★

Turning the knob on the door of Cecily's sitting-room was one of the hardest things Vicki had ever done. She felt like Alice stepping in through the looking-glass not knowing who she would meet. But it had to be done. She took a deep breath and went in!

Inside, the room looked cosy and welcoming. There was a log fire burning in the stone grate and a bowl of pink hyacinths on the table beside a chintz-covered chair. Even the brass had been highly polished and Vicki recognised that Cecily, not usually a houseproud lady, had made a special effort for this meeting.

Someone was in the chair but at the sound of the door opening he looked up and tried to leap chivalrously to his feet. Unfortunately the chair was deep and he began to struggle. So the first think Vicki ever said to her father was a hurried, 'Please, don't get up.'

To prevent any further struggles she went quickly to the sofa facing his chair and sat down. He settled again and she saw that there was a walking-cane beside him.

He held his head proudly, taking her survey with his chin held high, as though daring her to find him wanting. There was bitterness within her in the thought that they had no shared memories.

The bitterness was washed away, however, by compassion for the anxiety he was clearly experiencing at this emotional meeting.

He was the first to speak. 'My dear! It was kind of you to agree to see me.'

Vicki said bluntly, 'It wasn't kind, I was curious. I only found out the truth yesterday. I'm still in a state of shock.'

'I know. Poor child. What an upsetting thing to discover suddenly.'

They were silent a moment. Then he said, as though the words were forced out of him, 'I loved her, you know. But we had to part; anything else would have hurt too many people. She understood. It was our dilemma and we paid for it. And there was no intention to have you taken into her brother's family — not in the beginning.'

Vicki hugged to herself a secret satisfaction that he seemed to be a man of integrity — certainly of education. His voice was low and cultured as he continued sadly.

'Can you ever forgive us for bringing you into the world and yet not bringing you up?' He sounded deeply ashamed and looked straight into her face as he spoke.

Vicki gave a sharp intake of breath. She had missed the last few words he spoke, because, as he raised his eyes she saw, with a sense of total wonder, that his eyes were almost identical to the ones that had gazed out of her mirror at her for twenty-eight years!

She blurted out, 'Oh, gosh, your eyes are just like mine! It hadn't occurred to me to look for resemblances. Somehow it makes everything seem more real.'

Harold smiled.

'Does it? I hope so. For myself I still find it incredible that we're sitting here together talking. Seeing you has been my dearest wish, but I didn't dream that I would actually be able to meet you. I never had another daughter, you see. Two sons, now with sons of their own. But you were my only daughter.'

He was gazing at her steadily.

'Yes, you're right, you do have my eyes. And Cecily's wonderful colouring. Cecily has told me something of what you have gone through in the last twenty-four hours. Are you very unhappy?'

Vicki, honest as always, answered with the directness Harold remembered, with bitter-sweet nostalgia, as typical of the young Cecily.

'No, I'm not unhappy at all. I was. I thought my world had come to an end but now — something happened out of the blue — and I hope . . . I don't know . . . '

She broke off in some confusion and Harold smiled, saying wisely, 'The young man in the kitchen? He seemed very protective of you.'

'Did he?' She blushed. 'Yes, he's the reason.'

They both began to talk at once and then both laughed. As they eagerly continued, Vicki's first impression was turning into a joyous recognition of a father of whom she could be proud. He was interesting, amusing, trying hard in the short time they had left, to bring her into his past life and comprehend something of hers. True, there was an underlying air of melancholy, but that was inevitable in the circumstances.

By the time Cecily, followed closely by Zak, brought in a tea-tray and conversation became general, the father and daughter had reached a mutual understanding which, given more time, would, Vicki was sure, have developed into affection and respect. The tragedy was that they had no more time!

Later, when Zak announced the arrival of Harold's taxi, he was already on his feet. Zak held his coat for him and shook hands. The older man gazed up at him gravely. He said nothing but something in his drawn face impelled Zak to say, 'I will take care of her — of them both. Trust me.'

Harold's taut expression relaxed slightly.

'I do, my boy. Though God knows I haven't any right to ask, considering what kind of father I've been.'

'Enough of that talk,' Cecily said brusquely, and he took her arm to walk to the car.

With her beside him he turned, propping himself against the side of the cab, in order to hold out both arms to Vicki.

'Goodbye, my child. I can't tell you how grateful I am to have met my daughter — and received her forgiveness. May you always be happy.'

Even up to the moment of parting, Vicki herself had been unprepared for the surge of grief which washed over her. It seemed the deepest of the ironies that she should, in one short hour, discover both the pleasure and pain of finding, and losing, a parent that she passionately wanted to get to know better.

'I'll never forget you,' she whispered and then turned and fled back to Zak's waiting arms so that the last few minutes could be Cecily's.

It felt as though the strong arms around her were a symbol of a lasting refuge.

'I'm sorry,' she whispered. 'You must think me an idiot.'

'Far from it.' Zak looked down at her, a gentle look in his eyes. 'That's what love is for. Someone to laugh with and someone to cry with. If you hadn't been moved by what is happening here today, you wouldn't be the girl I've fallen in love with.'

When they heard the sound of the taxi departing, they both ran outside. Vicki rushed to one side of Cicely and Zak to the other. Together the three of them went back inside, arm in arm.

Once back in the cottage, though the tears were still running down Cecily's face, she quickly pulled herself together, and reverted to type.

'Just give me a little time,' she said gruffly. 'This belongs to the past. I did all my weeping for us long ago — and got on with life. I will again.'

'Of course you will.' Vicki was quick to agree. Cecily was making for the stairs. 'Do you want me to come with you?'

'No, but thanks for the offer. I need to be alone for a little bit.' She sniffed, blew her nose on a man's handkerchief and said through it, in a slightly muffled voice, 'You two go and sit on the sofa and sort yourselves out.'

'Yes, ma'am.'

Zak grinned at her disappearing back, took Vicki's still reluctant hand and drew her into the sitting-room.

'I shouldn't leave her,' Vicki said worriedly.

'Yes, you should. She's spent the major part of her life alone, and she prefers to give way to her feelings in private.' Zak was firm on that point.

'I suppose you're right.'

Vicki allowed herself to be pulled down on the sofa. Zak put his left arm around her shoulder and with his right, took her chin between thumb and forefinger.

Vicki, reading his intention, said, 'Please, don't kiss me. It doesn't seem right when Cecily is so unhappy upstairs.'

Zak sighed. 'How am I going to convince you that that is exactly what she had in mind? Nothing would please her more. 'Sort yourselves out,' she said, if you recall. And that's exactly what I'm trying to do.'

Vicki's lips twitched, but she put up a hand and placed it delicately in front of his mouth.

'No, you're not to kiss me yet! Once you do that I can't think straight.'

Zak said soulfully, 'I can't think straight already — not with you so close.'

He removed the hand and kissed her forehead, the tip of her nose, one cheek, then the other.

Vicki, acutely aware of his actions, did her best to pretend they were having no effect on her. She spoke thoughtfully.

'I've been thinking about my future plans. I've come to the conclusion it would be best for me to make a fresh start completely away from the island.'

'That's too bad. I wish you'd told me before.' He was kissing her ears through her thick mane of hair, first one than the other. 'Because I've more or less decided to buy a place here — as a holiday home we can come back to whenever we feel like it.'

The 'we' sounded delicious but she was not going to be taken for granted that easily. Trying to inject a haughty distance into her voice she said, 'I can't recall being asked, or agreeing, to share your life.'

Zak, having kissed as much as he could easily reach, was closing in on her temptingly-near lips. His mouth touching hers, he whispered, 'I apologise for the oversight, Miss Jamieson. This position is amazingly comfortable and I should really prefer not to go down on one knee. So will you excuse me if I stay where I am and just say, 'Darling Vicki, will you marry me?' '

Without waiting for her answer, he resisted temptation no longer and allowed their mouths to meet.

Vicki knew, for the second time in her life, the starbursting pleasure of the beginnings of passion, love and trust. And it was just a beginning, she reminded herself silently. We have our whole lives to find out what a real marriage of mind, body and spirit can provide.

*　*　*

When they drew apart, breathless, to look into each other's eyes and see the mutual love and desire reflected there, Cecily was standing beside them, smiling. How long she had been there, neither of them knew.

'Well, you seem to have sorted it all

out satisfactorily,' she said in a matter-of-fact tone.

'Now that,' Zak pronounced, with a laugh, 'is the understatement of the year. Magnificently, stupendously, incredibly, amazingly, fantastically, yes — but satisfactorily . . . Anyway, she hasn't said she'll marry me yet.'

Cecily made short work of this slight objection.

'Of course she'll marry you,' she announced. 'Tell him so. Put him out of his misery, Vicki.'

For answer, Vicki looked demurely up at Zak. For all his sophistication and worldly-wise air, there was still a hint of apprehension in his expression. Did he really think she would refuse?

An imp of mischief entered into her.

'Oh, all right, then, I suppose I'd better agree,' she said demurely, adding teasingly, 'But just remember, when we're standing at the altar, that I only said 'yes' to keep the peace — and to please my mother.'

SUMMER IN HANOVER SQUARE

Charlotte Grey

The impoverished Margaret Lambart is suddenly flung into all the glitter of the Season in Regency London. Suspected by her godmother's nephew, the influential Marquis St. George, of being merely a common adventuress, she has, nevertheless, a brilliant success, and attracts the attentions of the young Duke of Oxford. However, when the Marquis discovers that Margaret is far from wanting a husband he finds he has to revise his estimate of her true worth.